PENGU
THE POWER

SWAMI MUKUNDANANDA is a world-renowned spiritual teacher from India and an international authority on mind management. He earned his degrees from the prestigious IIT Delhi and IIM Calcutta but chose to renounce a promising corporate career and embrace monkhood. He studied Vedic scriptures at the feet of Jagadguru Kripaluji Maharaj. For almost four decades now, Swami Mukundananda has been sharing his vast knowledge through his books, lectures, and life-transformation programmes.

Swamiji meets hundreds, even thousands, of people every day from all walks of life. His steadfast positivity exudes hope, clarity, and a sense of purpose for those who connect with him. He has deeply affected the lives of millions of people who have been drawn to his profound integrity, charismatic personality, and passion to serve. Those who meet him experience his genuine care, and compassionate personality, and also feel deeply touched by him.

Swamiji's lectures are humorous, his arguments logical and well-laid-out, and, most of all, his advice is practical. His lectures on social media platforms are loved and followed by millions. Swamiji divides his time between India and the US.

ADVANCE PRAISE FOR THE BOOK

'Swami Mukundanandaji's books are life-changing. *The Power of Thoughts* just takes Swamiji's magical ability to blend science, wisdom and spiritual narratives with real-life application to another level. As I read through this treasure of knowledge, I could apply the powerful concepts included inside with immediate effect. This is a gem'—Alok Kejriwal, CEO and co-founder, Games2win and bestselling author

'In the evolving knowledge economy, this book provides invaluable insights into the power of thoughts and how they attract circumstances to us. Plus, valuable tips on how to improve our inner factory of thoughts. A beautiful blend of Vedic wisdom with neuro-physiological-psychological theory, taught through unforgettable stories'—Harish Rangacharya, CEO, Apex Group, Virginia, USA

'Swami Mukundananda has been writing and speaking on mind management for many years. His latest book, *The Power of Thoughts*, is a valuable addition to the literature on the crucial role that our thoughts play in moulding our consciousness. I warmly commend him on this book which, I am sure, will be of real help to those on the spiritual path'—Padma Vibhushan Dr Karan Singh, philosopher and ex-central cabinet minister

'This is not just a book; this is the voice in your head. Every day you are alone with your thoughts, but most of us do not pay attention to them. Swami Mukundananda is a change-maker in every sense. In this book, he distils the essentials of the mind and how we can work on our thoughts for creating the future we want. His work is full of ideas, tools and questions that will guide you to a better future' —Payal Nanjiani, executive coach, leadership speaker, author of *Success is Within*

'This book is a revelation and a true *marg darshan* for this generation and many more to come. In this digitally controlled world where we barely get the time to sit back and think, this book will help us to grapple with our thoughts, if not fully control them, thereby leading to a path that can engender a more meaningful life. This book has provided me instant gratification as it is not only going to make my personal life better but also make me a more disciplined and successful artist'—Devesh Mirchandani, Bollywood choreographer, artist and dance instructor

'His strategies to unleash your thinking shall enable you to achieve great breakthroughs in your life and live your life to the fullest. This book is strongly recommended for all those who want to take the trajectory of their life to the next level. A must-read'—Wg Cdr Namrita Chandi (Retd), international motivational speaker and bestselling author

'Swami Mukundanandaji's book is both scientific as well as spiritual in nature. From the scholarship of ancient Indian wisdom to research in modern science, he gets us into the world of thoughts from a higher perspective. The book is going to change your understanding of the mind, intellect and brain forever. It's a must-read for scientists and spiritual seekers equally'—Dr Radhakrishnan Pillai, leadership trainer and bestselling author

'This thought-provoking book provides insights on guiding principles that will help you get more out of life, shrug off adversity more easily, and generally be a happier, calmer and more fulfilled person'—Gp Capt. R. Vijayakumar (Retd), executive director, Madras Management Association

'Swami Mukundananda's work, besides being insightful, is also extremely inspirational. If you are struggling with the way things are in your life and clamouring for a change, look no further. This book provides you the foundation to begin that change yourself and take charge of your destiny'—Dr Vineet Agarwal, physician and bestselling author of *Vishwamitra* and *The Legend of Parshu-Raam*

THE
POWER OF
THOUGHTS

From the author of the bestselling
THE SCIENCE OF MIND MANAGEMENT

SWAMI
MUKUNDANANDA

PENGUIN
ANANDA

An imprint of Penguin Random House

PENGUIN ANANDA

USA | Canada | UK | Ireland | Australia
New Zealand | India | South Africa | China

Penguin Ananda is part of the Penguin Random House group of companies
whose addresses can be found at global.penguinrandomhouse.com

Published by Penguin Random House India Pvt. Ltd
4th Floor, Capital Tower 1, MG Road,
Gurugram 122 002, Haryana, India

First published in Penguin Ananda by Penguin Random House India 2022

Copyright © Radha Govind Dham, Delhi 2022

10 9 8 7 6 5 4 3 2 1

ISBN 9780143452331

Typeset in Sabon by Manipal Technologies Limited, Manipal

www.penguin.co.in

This book is dedicated to my beloved Spiritual Master, Jagadguru Shree Kripaluji Maharaj, the embodiment of divine love and grace, who illuminated humankind with the purest rays of divine knowledge. He was immersed in the highest bliss of divine love and engaged in inundating the entire planet with it. I am eternally indebted to him for bestowing upon me his divine wisdom and for inspiring me to consecrate my life to its propagation. I pray that by his blessings this book will help sincere seekers appreciate and manifest the power of their thoughts.

Contents

Introduction

We all wish to build a great destiny for ourselves and create fabulous circumstances in our life. We long to be happier in our attitudes, to be more effective at work. But where do we begin this process of change? What resources do we require for transforming ourselves? Where can we find them? And how much will those life-enhancing assets cost us?

It may surprise you to know that the ingredients for initiating a hugely successful life cost nothing at all. In fact, we already mass-produce more than 60,000 of them every day. The problem is that their quality is appalling and the quantity uncontrolled. If only we could learn to create them better, and in the right amount, they would enhance every aspect of our lives.

I am referring to our thoughts. Everything we do and experience begins with thinking. If our thoughts are virtuous, energetic and joyous, we perforce develop a noble character and perform heroic actions. Conversely, when we allow our mind to delve on immoral, abject and bitter emotions, we unavoidably set ourselves up for a wretched existence.

Very few people in the world pay attention to this sequence of causation. They grapple with improving their actions, only to see their developmental efforts undone by impure thoughts. If they had instead focused on transforming their thinking, even a fraction of their efforts would have yielded incredible results.

The ramifications of our thoughts also extend to our physical countenance. Wicked and hateful thoughts chisel our face, as ruthless sculptors, leaving lasting scars for all to see. Likewise, kind and loving thoughts work as the best possible beauty aids and are completely organic too! This is the reason behind the old maxim: 'the face is the index of the mind'.

In recent times, the Benson-Henry Institute for Mind Body Medicine at Massachusetts General Hospital has done ground-breaking research in scientifically establishing the relationship between thoughts and health.[1] Their studies have only confirmed what India's holy books of wisdom stated many millennia ago. Our thoughts generate chemical responses in the

---

[1] 'Mission & History', Benson-Henry Institute, accessed 3 August 2020, https://bensonhenryinstitute.org/mission-history/

body. Thus, resentful, jealous and odious thoughts do not come without a cost. They lower our vitality and set us up for a variety of physical ailments, such as allergies, autoimmune disorders, diabetes, cardiac issues, irritable bowel syndrome and ulcers.[2] Emotions management is thus an inseparable part of the holistic approach to health.

Since every aspect of our life experience is so strongly linked to the quality of our thoughts, it becomes necessary to comprehend them in greater depth. How are they created, and in what way are they different from gross objects? Why do some thoughts repeatedly come to our mind? And how can we alter our thinking patterns?

For thousands of years, elevated sages and yogis made these questions the subject of their study. Working in the laboratory of their own mind and intellect, they discovered some astonishing truths about Creation. They learnt why happy and sad thoughts arise. How thoughts transform into cravings. The harm that impure thoughts cause. And the benefits that accrue from purifying them.

---

[2] 'The Herbert Benson, MD Course in Mind Body Medicine', Harvard Medical School, accessed 3 August 2020, https://mindbody. hmscme.com/?utm_source=harvard-online-learning&utm_medium=referral&utm_campaign=ce-hoc

All this led them to conclude that the entire cosmos is receptive to our thoughts. In fact, the grand scheme behind the design of the Universe is to help souls evolve to divine heights. As a virtuoso sculptor, Life is intent on making masterpieces of us. Therefore, when we strive to grow from within, we align ourselves with the highest purpose of our life.

Inner growth is all about transforming our thoughts. The deepest work in this field was again done by the great rishis and ascetics of yore. Through austerities and self-discipline, while residing in the snow-capped Himalayas and its secluded caves, they perfected immensely powerful tools for revolutionizing their faculties of thought. That expertise was passed down in sacred books of wisdom.

It was almost half a century ago—while I was yet in middle school—that I began studying and practising the science of thoughts. During my journey, I had the good fortune of receiving one-on-one guidance from a most amazing, descended Saint. He shared with me the esoteric secrets of mind-mastery and oversaw my practise of them. He then entrusted me with the task of disseminating the same knowledge for the benefit of others. As I strived in my humble way to serve, I experienced how my divine guide had made me His instrument for touching the lives of millions all over the world.

The book in your hands is written with the sincere aspiration of explaining the ancient science of the mind and intellect in a modern context with present-day scientific research, real-life examples, humorous stories, sound logic and verses from sacred texts. I hope it will enable you to utilize the immense energy of your emotions to make your life healthier, happier and more successful.

The *Power of Thoughts* has two parts. In the first half, I have dealt with thoughts that harm us and techniques for eradicating or sublimating them. In the second half, I have explained strategies to unleash your thinking to live life to the fullest.

I hope you have a magnificent and enlightening journey as we proceed together through the pages of this book.

Swami Mukundananda

1

Let Us Think about Thoughts

The world in which we live is subtler than meets the eye. The air around us is replete with hundreds of types of electromagnetic waves. We cannot see them, but they are ever-present. If we switch on a radio and begin scanning the frequencies, it plays one station after another. How does this happen? The electromagnetic signals from various stations are present in the atmosphere. The radio picks them up.

These waves are a form of energy. From the Vedic perspective, the entire universe is a conglomeration of vibrating energy (shakti). Our perception of matter as consisting of solid objects is misleading. If we were to descend to the subatomic level, we would find that there are no tangible entities. What seems to us as solid matter is composed of pulsating patterns of energy. Based on how the energy vibrates, it acquires physical properties and gets classified as earth, water, fire, air or space.

Our thoughts are energy forms too, but of a very subtle kind, even subtler than the electromagnetic spectrum. These are the ideas, plans and opinions we generate in the factory of our mind, and they impact every aspect of our life.

Thoughts Affect the Environment

Though thoughts are subtle, the power they contain is immense. Saints who have mastered their mind are able to release thought waves of love, peace and compassion that influence everyone around them. Consider the following example.

A saintly person lived in a cave in the lofty Himalayas. Near his mountainous dwelling was a tranquil lake, frequented by gorgeous white swans, called rāj haṅs. The holy man loved the serenity of the lakeside. It was his favoured location for morning meditation and evening prayers. While he sat there, soaking in the harmony of nature, he blended in beautifully with the environment. The swans would fearlessly venture to just an arm's distance away from where he sat.

One day, an ornithologist happened to witness this spectacle. He was hoping to capture a couple of these rare birds for a public exhibition. However, the moment they saw him thirty metres away, they would fly off. So, he requested the saint, 'I desperately need your help in catching the rāj haṅs. Please allow them to come close, and then grab them for me.'

Pressed by the ornithologist, the gentle saint again sat by the lakeside the next morning. He closed his eyes, as if meditating, but his intention was to catch the birds. At intervals of a few minutes, he would open his eyes to see if any bird was at arm's length. However, to his astonishment, the morning went by, and no swan ventured close to him.

What had changed? It was his thoughts. Earlier, while meditating, he would emanate vibrations of love and kindness. The birds would intuitively perceive his goodness and approach him fearlessly. But this time, the evil intent in his heart had affected his psychological waves. Realizing this, the swans stayed away instinctively.

This is an example of our thought vibrations affecting the environment around us. Similarly, they affect places as well. When we walk into a house of worship, we naturally experience the hush of peace and a surge of pious sentiments. That is because tens of thousands of devotees have prayed there, and the energy of the place has changed.

On the other hand, on visiting a slaughterhouse, we will experience the reverse energy. Our spirit will droop, thoughts will become heavy and emotions morose. Why? The mental anguish of the thousands of animals killed there is lodged in the building. Our mind will pick it up and perceive the dreariness.

The following episode from the Puranas highlights this phenomenon.

Shravan Kumar is renowned in Indian history for his obedience to his parents. They were blind and old, yet he served them dutifully. When they needed to travel, he would seat each in a basket tied to either end of a bamboo pole. Holding the bamboo pole across his shoulders, he would carry them lovingly to their desired destination.

Nonetheless, a time came when even the dutiful Shravan rebelled. At one place in the forest of Dandakaranya, he set down the bamboo pole and complained, 'Enough is enough. How long can I bear the tiresome load of both of you?'

Shravan's father realized they were at the spot where Soorpanakha, a demoness, had once lived before moving elsewhere. Residues of her unholy vibrations were still affecting the place and had corrupted their son's intellect. 'Just take us a little further,' the father said. 'Then, if you wish, you can abandon us.'

When they walked away from the area, Shravan's intellect was cleared up and his filial devotion revived. He continued serving his parents with reverence.

In the above story, Soorpanakha's unholy thoughts had poisoned the habitat. When we progress in sadhana, we can decouple our thoughts from the environment. After all, the Supreme is all-pervading in the world. Therefore, good spiritual practitioners are able to keep their consciousness elevated, wherever they may be. Nevertheless, Shravan's episode illustrates the interconnectedness between thoughts and the environment.

Next, let us see the power of thoughts on our physique.

Thoughts Can Heal or Poison Our Body

We all take the utmost care not to ingest poison in any form. Yet, at times we do so unknowingly. It may be through the canned food we eat or the bottled water we drink.

In 2002, there was an uproar in India over the presence of pesticides in bottled water. The Pollution Monitoring Laboratory of the Centre for Science and Environment (CSE) analysed different brands of plastic bottled water. This led to a startling revelation. The prestigious Bisleri water contained 7900 per cent more pesticide content than the stipulated limit!

Bisleri did take corrective action subsequently and, since then, the Indian government too has implemented strict laws to protect people from poisonous chemicals. However, we remain oblivious of the large amounts of poison that pour into our blood and organs due to negative thoughts. **Fear, hostility, envy and resentment—all these adversely affect the body. Thought poisons are subtle, but their consequences can be grave.** Let me share my own experience with the mind-body connection.

As a spiritual counsellor and wellness teacher with many decades of experience, I am repeatedly asked for advice on a variety of medical ailments. Wherever my knowledge and experience permit, I do oblige with guidance on yoga, pranayam, nutrition and mind management.

Over the years, as I counselled people, I began to notice that those who complained of acute arthritis were also holding on to undue hostility. They had a resentful nature and were nurturing a grudge in their heart. Could there be a connection?

Then, in a chance meeting, I got an opportunity to test my hypothesis. On a morning walk in Delhi, I met a couple who had previously been active devotees of our satsang.

'I have not seen you both for a year now,' I said. 'Why do you no longer participate?'

'Swamiji, my wife is very unwell,' replied the husband. 'She has severe arthritis.'

I then asked his wife, 'Are you nurturing excessive hostility?'

'Oh Swamiji!' the husband interjected. 'You hit the nail on the head. She is full of bitterness and refuses to let go of her grudges.'

At that point, the lady spoke up. 'Swamiji, you are very right. The day my feelings of animosity increase, the pain in my body aggravates. However, now that you have pointed it out, I will try my best to avoid bitter thoughts.'

Medical science informs us that arthritis can develop for a hundred different reasons. However, studies at John Hopkins University have established that the pain experienced by arthritic patients is exacerbated when they harbour hostile feelings towards someone.[1] So, resentful thoughts may not be the cause for arthritis, but they can aggravate the symptoms.

Similarly, excessive anxiety impedes the proper functioning of our digestive system. It is a major cause for ulcers, acidity and irritable bowel syndrome.[2]

---

[1] 'Yoga Improves Arthritis Symptoms and Mood, Study Finds', John Hopkins Medicine, accessed 28 July 2020, https://www.hopkinsmedicine.org/news/media/releases/yoga_improves_arthritis_symptoms_and_mood_study_finds

[2] 'Diseases and Conditions. The Gut-Brain Connection', Harvard Health Publishing, Harvard Medical School, 19 April 2021, https://www.health.harvard.edu/diseases-and-conditions/the-gut-brain-connection

Likewise, grief saps the body of energy. It leads to fatigue and weakness of the muscles.[3] In the same manner, excessive worry depresses our immune system, making us susceptible to colds, flu, diseases and infections.[4]

The Vedic scriptures give the reason for this. They explain that harbouring mental poisons disturbs the smooth and regular flow of prana (vital energy). The disturbance in *pranic shakti* disorganizes the *nādis* (energy channels within the body), as a result of which some receive more than normal energy, while others get less. Such an imbalanced state over time leads to disease.

Modern research on the mind-body connection is validating the Vedic perspective. Study after study is revealing that extreme hatred, bitter jealousy and numbing anxiety are all harmful to our body. They injure the cells in our kidneys, heart, intestines and liver. In this way, toxic thoughts become the cause of disease. The word 'dis-ease' itself means 'lack of ease', or dearth of mental harmony.

---

[3] 'Grief Can Have Very Real Physical Symptoms', Pathways Health, accessed 15 December 2020, https://pathwayshealth.org/grief-support/grief-can-have-very-real-physical-symptoms/

[4] Dr Saul McLeod, 'Stress, Illness and the Immune System', Simply Psychology, Updated 2010, https://www.simplypsychology.org/stress-immune.html

Conversely, our health and well-being are enhanced when we feel joyous. Positive thoughts of love, hope and courage are the best vitamins we can offer our body. They nourish our organs and rejuvenate our energy levels. Not surprisingly, as per Ayurveda, the most effective way to bring our kapha, pitta and vatta into balance is to cultivate selfless love in our heart.

About 2500 thoughts run through our mind every hour. Imagine their potential healing power if they are joyous and optimistic. A popular Sanskrit prayer states:

> *sarve bhavantu sukhinaḥ*
> *sarve santu nirāmayāḥ*
> *sarve bhadrāṇi paśhyantu*
> *mā kaśhchid duḥkhabhāg bhavet*
> *om śhāntiḥ śhāntiḥ śhāntiḥ*

'May all beings be happy; may everyone be healthy and well. May auspiciousness come to us from all sides; and may no one suffer. Om peace . . . peace . . . peace.'

The beautiful idea behind the prayer is to train our mind to nurture compassionate and noble emotions.

Thoughts Determine Our Happiness and Distress

Shakespeare had said, 'There is nothing either good or bad but thinking makes it so.' I once witnessed an eye-opening example of this statement.

In June 2013, there was devastating flooding in the north Indian state of Uttarakhand. It was caused by cloudbursts, followed by excessive rains. Landslides due to the floods damaged several buildings. Debris from the hills jammed the rivers and increased the deluge.

When news of the calamity spread, aid poured in from around the world. At JKYog, we too launched a drive to help. However, what became permanently etched in my memory was a scene I saw on TV. A television crew was conducting on-the-spot interviews. Harried residents were sharing their tales of woe, when the camera suddenly turned to an old woman.

The interviewer asked her, 'Māji (Mother), what has been your tragedy?'

'I am so thankful to God,' the old woman responded.

'Do you mean there has been no damage to your home?' the puzzled reporter queried.

'No. In fact, my home has been washed away,' replied the old woman.

'Then why are you thanking the Lord?'

'I am grateful to Him because my husband is alive, and my children and grandchildren are safe. The house can be built again, but if any of my family members

had died, the loss would have been irreplaceable. I feel blessed that they are still with me.'

Watching the coverage, I wished I could have touched the woman's feet. As per Government of Uttarakhand reports, more than 5700 people were 'presumed dead' in the deluge. Yet, in the midst of death and destruction, this woman was brimming with positivity, hope and contentment.

What was her secret? Simply the way she chose to think. The circumstances were grim; but rather than brooding over her loss, she focused on the silver lining she saw in the situation. It did not cost her more to think positively, but it made such a difference to her inner joy.

In the US, the woman's thinking style would be called 'positive reframing'. Psychologists charge up to $200 an hour to coach clients in it. The poor old woman did not have the benefit of such training, yet she had proved a golden truth: **Our experience of happiness and distress is not dependent on circumstances, but the way we look at them.**

Though the outer world is objective, it enters our consciousness through the lens of our mind. Hence, our perception of the objective world is subjective. When people are unhappy, they blame external circumstances for it. But if they simply changed their viewpoint, their experience of misery would also change.

Dinesh comes to office on Monday. 'I am so happy,' he tells his colleagues. 'God's infinite grace is upon me.'

'What happened?' they all ask eagerly. 'Did you win a lottery?'

'No, I had an accident while riding my motorbike,' responds Dinesh. 'A crazy guy brushed past my bike with his speeding car. I lost my balance and hit an electric pole. The X-ray revealed my thumb was fractured.'

'What?! You had an accident, and you are still thanking God?'

'Yes, the way that guy was driving his car, he could have killed me. I am lucky I got away with a small fracture.'

Notice how sagacious Dinesh's thinking is. His thumb is already broken. If he keeps brooding over it, he will feel miserable, but it will not help him in any way because the damage is already done. As the saying goes, 'There is no use crying over spilt milk'. Instead, Dinesh has reframed the accident in a positive light. By choosing his thoughts well, he is cheerful. In an identical situation, most others would have felt a spate of negative emotions, such as self-pity and bitterness.

The moral of the story is: **we become happy or sad by the thoughts we bring to our mind.** Then why do we not think good thoughts more often? Because we have not truly realized their importance. So, let us appreciate more deeply why thoughts are so crucial to the quality of our life.

Our Thoughts Define Us

It is straightforward logic. Good people are those who primarily think compassionate and chaste thoughts. Conversely, bad people are those whose thoughts are mostly spiteful and capricious. Verily, our thoughts determine the level of our consciousness. The story of a priest and the prostitute elucidates this principle.

Once upon a time, a prostitute moved into the house adjoining a priest's home. This led to a lot of tension. The priest would chant sacred mantras from the holy scriptures but the events at his neighbour's residence disturbed him. There was a steady stream of men entering the prostitute's home in the evenings and night. If the priest happened to wake up at midnight, he would still find men walking in and out of her home.

Finally, unable to control his exasperation, he accosted the courtesan. 'Do you not realize the gravity of the sins you are committing? You will not even get a place in hell.'

The poor woman trembled to her bones on hearing the priest's moral chastisement. She rued the profession she was stuck in. Yet, being uneducated and poor, she knew of no other means of livelihood. With profound regret, she continued her trade. However, she would always admire the holy life of the priest because he would read the scriptures and engage in worship rites. She prayed for the day when she too could change her life.

On the other hand, the priest's attention was getting diverted from God. Every time he saw a customer visiting his neighbour, he would take a stone and add it to the pile in his garden. In time, it grew into a heap. One day, he screamed at the prostitute again, 'You wretched woman! I am keeping an account of your sins.'

The poor courtesan became even more terrified. She prayed to God with greater earnestness for redemption from her sinful life.

As fate would have it, the two of them died on the same day. In her next life, the courtesan was born in a pious family, in line with her deepest aspirations.

The priest, however, was taken to the nether regions. When he asked why he had received such a fate after a lifetime of pious activity, he was informed, by the Lord of Death, 'You were performing ritualistic practices only as a physical drill, while in your mind you constantly dwelt upon the prostitute.'

The message is clear. Holiness cannot be measured by the clothes we wear, the mantras we chant or the place we live in. The true gauge of our piety is always our thoughts. Saint Kabir stated it so poignantly:

prem bhāv ek chāhiye, bheṣh anek banāy
chāhe ghar meṅ vās kare, chāhe van meṅ jāy

'The important thing is to nurture loving sentiments. What you wear and where you reside—whether at home or in the forest—is irrelevant.'

Similarly, Jagadguru Kripaluji Maharaj stated in his composition, *Bhakti Śhatak*:

bandhan aur mokṣh kā, kāraṇ manahi bakhān
yāte kauniu bhakti karu, karu man te haridhyān

(verse 19)

'Bondage in maya or liberation from it, is determined by the state of our mind. Hence, whatever form of devotion you practise, do ensure that, alongside, you meditate upon the Supreme.'

The Buddha had declared twenty-five centuries ago: 'All that we are is the result of what we have thought.' His words have an immensely powerful implication that our present was forged by our past thoughts, and our future will be forged by our present ones.

That is why all authentic mystical systems of spirituality focus on inner transformation. This entails eliminating materialistic thoughts and replacing them with divine ones. For that purpose, they use methods, such as introspection, contemplation, meditation and sublimation.

Thoughts Are Precursors to Actions

Every action we perform is preceded by a thought. Whether we brush our teeth, eat a meal or chit-chat with friends, there is always a thought that generates the impulse for it.

Hence, the kinds of thoughts we cultivate in our mind create the basis for our actions. **Great personalities who enhanced the lives of millions were able to do so because they empowered their thoughts with purity and energized them with vigour.** The monumental work they accomplished in life was a natural consequence.

If we aspire to emulate these shining luminaries, and if we wish to perform noble deeds and heroic acts, then we too must uplift our thinking. Suppose we wish to do spectacular work, but our emotions are miserable, how will we ever succeed? **The formula for success is that we rise in life by elevating our thoughts.**

A little boy, Chandu, accompanied his mother to a Diwali mela. His young mind was thrilled by the numerous fascinations there. However, what really grabbed his imagination was a balloon stall.

The balloon seller had a bunch of helium balloons in different colours. To attract people's attention, every once in a while he would release a balloon in the air. Chandu would gaze in amazement as the balloon defied gravity and drifted towards the stratosphere.

Chandu witnessed a yellow balloon go up, followed by a red one and then a green one. Unable to contain his curiosity, he asked the seller, 'Sir, if you release the black balloon, will it also float that high?'

'Son,' responded the seller. 'The colour of the balloon does not decide how high it floats. It's what's inside it that matters.'

Similarly, **how high we rise in life is charted by the level of thoughts we harbour within**.

And it does not stop at that. Others too derive inspiration from our elevated emotions. Swami Vivekananda, it seems, understood this principle deeply. Prior to his epoch-making journey to the US, he wrote that he would lift his mind to such heights so as to inspire people everywhere, until the world realized that it was one with God.

Historically, Indian culture has laid great emphasis on inner wealth, and those who possess it are offered the highest respect in society. That is why Adi Shankaracharya asked a question in his book, *Prashnavali*:

jagad jitaṁ kena?

'Who shall achieve victory in the world?'

The answer he provided was:

mano hi yena

'Those who have conquered their own mind.'

It is highly probable that, like Shankaracharya and Vivekananda, you too realize the importance of training your thoughts. That is why you have chosen to read this book. But the difference is that you are probably unaware of the techniques and have not implemented them yourself.

This chapter was dedicated to appreciating the power of thoughts. As we progress from chapter to chapter, we will learn the practices for manifesting their potential in a sequential manner. First, we will learn the means to eliminate negative emotions. Subsequently, we will discuss the creation of positive thoughts.

2

Watch Your Thoughts

The biggest obstacle to tapping into the power of thoughts is lack of control over them. Imagine sitting for a meal and having no ability to choose what we put in our mouth. If we were fed pickles and vinegar repeatedly and randomly, what a ridiculous situation would be created! Unfortunately, that is how it is with thoughts. Rather than us selecting the ones we want, they come on their own accord, as uninvited guests.

The consequence? Our poor intellect gets riddled with wretched and worthless ideas that add no value. This has to be reversed—we must be able to choose the emotions that work for us. Then alone can we adopt thoughts that empower and reject ones that hinder us.

The pity is that not many of us know how to select our thoughts. We tell our hand to comb our hair, and it obeys. It works under our command. If, instead, the hand responded by scratching the head, it would become a daft situation, where nothing worthwhile could ever be done. But when it comes to the mind, it seems to work according to an algorithm of its own. Most thoughts seem to arrive as gatecrashers and take residence without our permission.

Fed up with his sentiments, an acquaintance said to me, 'Swamiji, my mind loves to work overtime on the weekends, even without pay.' So precisely expressed! Unlike our hands and feet, why does the mind not respond to our commands, and how can we make it do so? Read on to know the answer.

The Victim Mentality

Every day I meet people who complain about the way they feel. They dislike the fact that miserable emotions overcome them. They find themselves besieged with fear, resentment and gloom. Sadly, the sentiments seem to clasp them so tightly that they refuse to dislodge.

A woman named Chanda (name changed) started volunteering at a JKYog satsang centre. Chanda was inspired to serve, which was praiseworthy, but there was a serious problem. Her mind was overactive in imagining the worst about everyone else. She would view even their innocent exchanges as the devil's intrigues.

If I tried defending others and explained that they were not so bad after all, it would annoy her even more.

'*You never believe me and only believe what others tell you,*' *she would respond.*

*One year turned out to be particularly painful for Chanda, and as a result, she reached a breaking point due to the perceived bad behaviour of others. Finally, she concluded with a climactic statement, '*When everyone is so bad, why should I not give up my seva?*'*

*I knew if I said even a single word in defence of anyone, she would accuse me of being prejudiced. Realizing the situation was sensitive, I responded, '*Chandaji, I accept that devotees have been unpleasant. However, I have only one question.* **Nobody is forcing you to think unhappy thoughts. Why have you chosen to make your mind negative?**'*

*Suddenly, her expression changed, as if the wind had been taken out of her arguments. Sensing her receptivity, I explained further, '*Agreed that people's behaviour was not the best possible but if you allowed your mind to be filled with bitterness, it was a mistake that you made.*'*

'*Chandaji,*' *I continued, '*If you wish to serve, I cannot guarantee a perfect environment because I cannot control people's behaviour. However, you are a spiritual practitioner; you should learn to control your own emotions. And the first step for that is to realize that you have the freedom to choose your own feelings.*'*

The poor woman was not alone in the mistake she was making. More than half of humanity falls prey to it. They think that someone's behaviour or a situation is responsible for the emotions they experience. The consequence is the 'victim mindset'. People who play the victim find justifications for their moods. 'My neighbour was rude to me', 'My child did not listen', 'The share market went down' and so on.

When we make excuses for emotions, our focus shifts away from self-improvement to self-pity. Consequently, we do not bother to manage our mind, which starts festering with negativity.

The Bondage of Emotions

As the Hindi saying states: *khālī dimāg, śhaitān kā ghar* 'An empty mind is a devil's abode'; it refuses to sit idle. If we do not consciously nurture progressive thoughts, our mind creates unproductive ones on its own. Stimuli from the environment make our emotions rise and fall. So, one event makes us angry, a second creates frustration, a third evokes anxiety, and so on. This becomes the roller coaster of our emotions.

The matter does not stop there, negative thoughts in the mind lead to a more serious problem. When a particular emotion is repeated multiple times, a neural pathway gets etched, and the brain gets conditioned to form an attitude. For instance, if we become irritable a few hundred times, the feeling of irritability gets locked in. It now develops into a really grave challenge. The brain's programming begins to control us.

At this stage, people perceive they are at the mercy of their feelings. They exclaim, 'I wish I were not so irritable' or 'Why do I always worry so much?' Now the mind has become their own worst enemy.

This whole chain started from the 'victim mentality' and resulted in the 'bondage of emotions'. How can we break this causation?

Stop Running on Autopilot

If we wish to prevent our mind from being an enemy, we must not allow it to run on autopilot. We are not obliged to accept the emotions that our mind presents to us. No matter what the external circumstances, we have the freedom to choose our response. Instead of compulsively rehashing problems in our mind, we must turn our attention towards available solutions. Focus on goals and methods to achieve them.

Take inspiration from a young Harvard alumnus, Liz Murray, a motivational speaker and winner of White House Project's Role Model Award.[1]

---

[1] 'Liz Murray: My parents were desperate drug addicts. I'm a Harvard graduate', Guardian, International Edition, accessed 10 June 2020, https://www.theguardian.com/world/2010/sep/26/liz-murray-bronx-harvard?

Liz grew up in the Bronx, a crime-infested part of New York. Her parents were alcoholics and drug addicts. They loved her but were preoccupied with drugs and had no time for her.

One morning, Liz woke up to discover that her parents had sold her sister's winter coat for money to purchase cocaine. To feed her sister and herself, Liz began working at a gas-station grocery store when she was only nine years old.

When she was fifteen, her mother died of AIDS and her father moved into a shelter home. Liz became homeless, but she took the experience in a positive light. She connected her parents' wretched lifestyle with its tragic consequences and decided that she would not allow her life to go down the same track.

First, she took a summer job without letting anyone know that she was homeless. Next, she got herself accepted at Humanities Preparatory Academy, a public school in Manhattan. To make up for time lost, she began taking double the number of classes. Her days would be spent in school and nights in subway trains.

She set her sights high and decided to apply to Harvard University and for the New York Times *scholarship. Her tenacity was tested when interviews for both fell on the same day. She walked away from the scholarship to attend her interview at Harvard. It paid off as she got selected by the premier university and also received the scholarship. Randy Kennedy of the* New York Times *observed that Liz completed four years of schooling in two and graduated at the top of her class of 158 students. It was an unheard of feat.*

Liz Murray summed it up like this: 'There's always a way through things if you work hard enough and look closely. It all depends on your level of determination.'

Notice that Liz Murray did not indulge in self-pity, 'Why did this happen to me?' Nor did she play the victim by creating excuses for negative thinking, 'My life is in a mess because of the lousy parents I got.' Instead, she took charge of her thoughts and powered them with positivity, determination and discipline.

Repeated studies have been conducted to understand what 'successful people' think and talk about and how they are different from the thought processes and conversations of 'failures'. The results reveal that unsuccessful people discuss problems and the persons they dislike. In contrast, successful people focus on goals and methods for achieving them. In the above story, Liz Murray demonstrated the thinking of effective people. We too must stop playing the victim and, instead, become the purposeful creators of our thoughts.

But why is it so difficult to create thoughts of our choice? Well, the reason our thoughts run on autopilot mode is that we do not even realize **we are not the mind; we are not our thoughts; and we are not our emotions.** Let us try and understand this.

We Are Not Our Thoughts

By themselves, thoughts are not harmful. They can enter our awareness and slip away, making scant difference to us. It is when we identify with them and see ourselves as 'the voice behind them' that the confusion begins, 'Why do I get immoral thoughts?' 'Why am I thinking of tragedies?' and so on.

One woman approached me. 'Swamiji, I gave birth to a sweet baby boy three months ago. But I have a big problem that I need to talk to you about.'

I told her to go ahead and tell me her problem.

'Swamiji, you will not believe what my mind thinks.'

I said, 'Does it involve the thought of slamming your baby against the wall?'

'Yes, how did you know?'

The unhappy mother had a typical problem. Consciously, she could never imagine doing anything nasty to her precious baby. But her mind was not under her control, and it had created a nasty thought. Rather than ignoring it, she had seen herself as the voice behind it and felt guilty. This had enlivened the thought further, and it was repeating itself.

It was like a self-reinforcing cycle that was puzzling her to no end. The more she hated the thought, the stronger it became. Her confusion was, 'Why am I thinking like this?'

Likewise, consider an even more disturbing but compulsive thought.

A gentleman once approached me and said, 'Swamiji, I really need to speak to you. I have a terribly serious problem.'

'Please go ahead and tell me,' I said.

'It is about the Divine Mother, Durga.'

'You have lewd thoughts about Her?'

'Oh my God! How did you know?'

The same problem as that of the new mother but even more guilt inducing! It probably so happened that the gentleman was having darshan of the Divine Mother's deity in the temple. Amongst the scores of thoughts that crossed his mind, one was lewd in nature. The matter would have ended in the next moment if he had allowed the thought to die its natural death. The mind would have passed its attention to other thoughts that were streaming in by the dozens.

The problem developed, however, when he saw himself as the creator of his thought. He identified with it and became riddled with guilt and confusion. Consciously, he would never ever want to think in such a manner. And yet, his mind was forcing him, contrary to his deepest values.

Both the new mother and the gentleman in the cases above had similar dilemmas, 'Why do I think this terrible thought?'

I gave the same answer to both. 'You are not thinking this thought.'

'Really!' there was a sudden reprieve on their faces. 'Then who is thinking it?'

'It is your mind that is thinking it, not you. The problem is that you are assuming you are the voice behind your thought, so it is getting strengthened. Stop associating with it. Distance yourself from it, and it will lose its grip on you.'

Most people confuse their mind to be themselves. The mind creates a happy thought, and they conclude, 'I am feeling joyous'. But the next moment, it produces an emotion of dismay, and they infer, 'I am feeling appalled'. In this way, the roller coaster of emotions continues.

There is, however, no compulsion to embrace every feeling that crosses our mind. We see birds flying in the sky and let them pass, without it affecting our consciousness. Likewise, we can distance ourselves from our thoughts by practising 'witness consciousness'. Let us understand this powerful technique.

Sākṣhī Bhav—Watch Your Thoughts

This is a methodology for distancing ourselves from and thereby neutralizing the grip of our negative thoughts. Compare it to surfing, a popular sport amongst beachgoers. They blissfully ride the waves on flat surfboards. Likewise, in *sākṣhī bhav*, we learn to surf our emotions and remain unaffected. It is based on the understanding of our true self.

The Bhagavad Gita explains the nature of the 'self', distinct from the mind:

> *apareyam itas tvanyāṁ prakritiṁ viddhi me parām*
> *jīva-bhūtāṁ mahā-bāho yayedaṁ dhāryate jagat*
> (verse 7.5)

'Beyond My material energy, O mighty-armed Arjun, I have a superior energy. This is the embodied souls, who are the basis of life in this world.'

Hence, we are neither the body nor the mind; we are divine souls. Understanding our identity provides the key for weakening our negative emotions. Whenever a negative thought pops into the mind, remember that it is not you. Rather than adopting it, you can distance yourself from it: 'Oh, my mind is playing mischief! I will not associate with this thought.' Slowly, you will establish a gap between yourself and your mind.

The beauty is that the moment we disidentify ourselves from thoughts, they lose power over us. In the Vedic tradition, this technique of watching our thoughts is called *sākṣhī bhav*. Here, *sākṣhī* means 'witness' and bhav means 'state of being'. Hence, *sākṣhī bhav* is a 'state of being the witness'. It refers to the practice of observing sensations in our mind and body without immediately reacting to them.

For example, on visiting a zoo, we delight in the varieties of animals we see there. Since the creatures are in their enclosures, we are safe. But if they were allowed out of their respective cages, a catastrophe would occur! Similarly, in witness consciousness, emotions exist, but we do not allow them to overpower us. If a feeling of irritation starts arising, we see the mind playing mischief, but we choose to remain a calm witness. Thus, we keep ourselves safe from the assault of emotions.

For enlightened saints, this witness mindset comes naturally. They do not need to tell themselves they are not the mind and body. They are already situated on the platform of self-realization. Hence, they can easily surf bodily and mental sensations.

Let me share some inspiring stories of such saints from recent times.

Ramana Maharshi (1879–1950) was a self-realized saint who lived in Tiruvannamalai, Tamil Nadu. In 1947, his health began to fail. The next year a small nodule appeared on his left arm. On seeing it grow, disciples called a surgeon from Chennai. He diagnosed it as osteosarcoma, a very painful form of bone cancer and declared the need for surgery.[2]

Sage Ramana was taken to the operating theatre where the preparations were complete. However, when it was time to administer the anaesthesia, Ramana Maharshi refused. He requested that the surgery be performed without it. The doctor kept the anaesthetist at hand and instructed him, 'The moment I cut into his hand and he starts screaming, give him the anaesthesia.'

The surgery was completed successfully and Ramana Maharshi remained calm throughout. Later, when questioned by the doctor about how he bore the pain, he responded, 'I was witnessing you cut into the arm, just as the attendants and nurses were.'

However, the surgery could not check the onslaught of the disease. Doctors suggested amputating his arm.

---

[2] 'Reminiscences', Om Namo Bhagavate Sri Ramanaya Sri Ramanasramam, accessed 30 June 2020, https://www.sriramanamaharshi.org/ramana-maharshi/reminiscences/

Again, Ramana Maharshi refused. 'There is no need to be alarmed,' he said. 'In any case, the material body is a bag of diseases. Why mutilate it? Let it come to its natural end.'

In witness consciousness, Ramana Maharshi watched the disease waste away his body. Though he was a divine personality, his body was material. It cannot be that he was free from pain, but he rode the sensation of pain, in *sākṣhī bhav*, like surfers ride the ocean waves.

There is a similarly extraordinary episode from the life of my Spiritual Master, Jagadguru Kripaluji Maharaj (1922–2013). When he was only thirty-four years old, the Kashi Vidvat Parishat conferred on him the title of 'Jagadguruttam', meaning 'the Supreme Spiritual Master of the World', in acknowledgement of his unparalleled mastery of the Vedic scriptures. He was lovingly called 'Maharajji' by his devotees.

Once Maharajji was in Kolkata for a lecture series when his appendix burst. Ordinarily, this would have been a life-threatening situation. However, he continued with his normal activities and the evening discourses. After two-and-a-half days, he mentioned to the devotees, 'I feel some discomfort on the side of my waist.' He was taken for a medical exam.

The doctor checked him and exclaimed, 'The fact that you are alive is a miracle. As per our medical books, you should be dead by now. We need to perform an immediate surgery to clean up the fluids that have spread in the abdomen.'

He was taken to the operating theatre. The anaesthetist gave him an injection, but it made no difference to him. The anaesthetist gave a second injection, and then a third, and yet, Maharajji remained in full awareness. He heard the doctors and attendants speaking to each other in hushed tones.

'What happened?' enquired Maharajji.

'To perform the surgery, we need you to be unconscious,' they explained. 'But the anaesthesia is having no effect on you.'

'How long do you need me to be unconscious?' asked Maharajji.

'Six hours,' they replied.

'Okay,' said Maharajji. 'I am going to sleep for six hours. I will wake up when the time is over. Please ensure the surgery is complete by then.'

He seemed to have gone off to sleep and then, after six hours, when the surgery was over, he came out of his feigned slumber.

These were of course extreme examples of divine personalities who possessed the ability to remain unaffected by physical pain. They had absolute realization that they were not their body and mind. Hence, the witness consciousness came naturally to them. We cannot emulate them at our present level of prowess, but we can surely inspire ourselves to work hard in that direction.

Dada Vaswani (1918–2018) was a very gentle and kind-natured saint. He was a champion of vegetarianism and animal rights. He was the spiritual leader of the Sindhi community around the world.

One of his followers related this incident about Dadaji to me when he spoke at the Millennium World Peace Summit of Religious and Spiritual Leaders, which was conducted at the United Nations. His talk was very well-received.

After the talk, his disciples complimented him, 'Dada, your discourse was incredibly eloquent and touching.'

'Yes, I was also listening,' replied Dada Vaswani, the personification of humility.

Dada Vaswani's statement revealed his elevated mindset. He was observing the articulate words emanating from his mouth. Yet, retaining witness consciousness, he was untouched by the pride of being the doer of his actions. He was aware of God's grace as it poured ideas into his head.

We too must strive to reach that level one day. But our practice will have to start at the beginning.

We must learn to become a witness to any harmful thoughts that pop up in our mind, and purposefully dissociate ourselves from them.

In recent times, the technique of 'mindfulness' has become popular in the West. It makes no mention of the 'self' as the divine soul, while the part about surfing the thoughts is retained. Mindfulness appeals to intellectuals and academicians as a kind of spirituality that does not require faith, devotion or surrender, and yet bestows enormous benefits in mind management.

Here, it is pertinent to mention that mindfulness is not an advanced spiritual practice. Rather, it is the gateway to enlightened living and the transcendental state. With its help, we can create a space between the self and the mind-body mechanism. This will help us achieve a measure of self-control, objectivity and equanimity. Then, we can progress to the techniques of thought refinement described in the subsequent chapters.

3

The Problem of Negative Thoughts

The previous chapter helped create a space between us and our mind. With that bit of freedom, we can now observe our thoughts and distinguish the beneficial from the harmful ones. In this chapter, we will learn why negative emotions arise and how to eliminate them.

Throughout the day, a multitude of thoughts of many different kinds, appear in our head. Some are cravings, while others are aversions. A few are ideas, while some are about things to do. These thoughts arouse feelings and emotions within us. A particular thought gives rise to fear, while another evokes reassurance. A third thought makes us sing in joy, and a fourth wince in misery. And each of these feelings can be of varying intensity, from mild to intense.

These thoughts and feelings make us recall memories. The memories evoke images, leading to further thoughts. This sets off a chain reaction of thoughts, feelings, memories and images, in a recurring manner. Sometimes the chain is within our control and works to our benefit. But very often, it is not. We find ourselves unable to manage our mind. It runs amok, causing us immense harm. Our own mental creations become unwanted monsters residing within.

Beware of Thought Poisons

Vāman Bhagavan had said, 'The enemies outside are tiny when compared to the demons living inside us. These are thoughts of lust, anger, greed, hatred and illusion.' The following story reveals just how dangerous these demons can be.

Howard Hughes (1905–1976)[1] was one of the most financially successful American business magnates of the twentieth century. He is listed as the forty-fourth richest man in history. Here are a couple of incidents that show the extent of his wealth. He once went to live in the penthouse suite of Desert Inn, a five-star hotel in Las Vegas. After many weeks, the manager got fed up and sought to evict him. Hughes purchased the hotel and then stayed on, since he was now the proprietor.

[1] Adapted from Donald L. Barlett and James B. Steele, *Howard Hughes: His Life and Madness*, W. W. Norton & Company, Inc., 2004, Kindle

He loved watching old movies on television, especially at night. In those days, there was no TV station in Las Vegas airing movies through the night. So, he purchased an existing station and got it to screen movies from the genre of his choice.

However, despite all his financial successes, he could not control his thoughts. In midlife, he developed a phobia of germs and a mania for secrecy. He believed he was free of microbes, but they would attack him from the outside. The dread of germs became an obsession. To protect himself, he would repeatedly clean his hands until they bled. While serving him, his staff had strict instructions to hold all cutlery in paper napkins, after having washed their hands three times. If any of his domestic helps fell sick, he would get scared of excessive germs in the house. Consequently, he would get his entire wardrobe burnt and replaced.

During the last two decades of his life, he frequently moved between hotels in Las Vegas, the Bahamas, Nicaragua, Canada, England and Mexico. His penthouse would be especially primed with black curtains and sealed windows. He considered them to be germ-free zones and would work in them, isolated from the harmful germs he believed were outside.

Though unimaginably wealthy, he spent his final days mentally imprisoned by his own horror of contamination and elaborate cleaning rituals. Intriguingly, he neglected his own hygiene and rarely bathed or brushed his teeth.

This is an example of someone who possessed tremendous opulence, and yet had a miserable quality of life. Obviously, the cause of his distress was not lack of wealth, power or fame. It was merely his inability to eliminate harmful thoughts.

The intricacies of the human mind are difficult to fathom, and so are the varieties of defective ideas it generates. Hughes's phobia of germs and mania for secrecy were just two examples of inner monsters created by faulty thinking. There are many more. Thousands of years ago, the Maharshi Patanjali stated in his *Yog Darshan*:

> *vitarkā hiṁsādayaḥ kṛitakāritānumoditā*
>   *lobhakrodhamohapūrvakā*
> *mṛidumadhyādhimātrā duḥkhajñānānantaphalā*
>   *iti pratipakṣhabhāvanam*   (sutra 2.34)

'Unwholesome thoughts can be of bitterness, untruth, etc. They come in three degrees—mild, moderate and intense. They can be created, instigated or approved, either because of avarice, anger or attachment.'

Let us see how these varieties of negative thoughts get scripted in our mind.

Why Negative Thoughts Arise

Have you ever felt about someone, 'This man does not know how to think'? Or have you come away from a discussion, sensing, 'She can't think straight'? Your estimation of the person could be true because faulty thought patterns are quite prevalent. In the previous story, Hughes' thinking was obviously defective. But what is it that creates faulty thinking in people?

Sometimes incorrect beliefs are the cause. Other times, it results from an erroneous way of looking at the world. While at times, it happens because of incomplete knowledge of things.

Maharshi Patanjali, it seems, was an absolute master in the science of thoughts. He stated the reasons for negative thinking:

viparyayo mithyājñānam atadrupa pratiṣhṭham
(*Yog Darshan* sutra 1.8)

'Misconceptions in thought (*viparyaya*) arise from erroneous knowledge. They occur while perceiving a thing as being other than what it really is.'

Erroneous knowledge, in turn, creates incorrect beliefs. Let us take a look at some of the most prevalent negative thought patterns and the fallacious beliefs from which they arise.

Overgeneralization

In this mode of thinking, we make a general assumption based on a single incident. For example, suppose Kavita does not like Rohit. Based on her rejection, Rohit concludes, 'No one likes me'. This statement is without sufficient basis. But Rohit firmly begins to believe that no one likes him. Now he looks at the world through the lens of this belief, and thinks, 'everyone dislikes me'.

Consider another example. Sandhya has failed in a job interview. So, she decides, 'I can never succeed at any interview'. Imagine how harmful these thoughts are to her career, but she is completely convinced about them.

Where we use the words 'all' or 'never', 'always' or 'none', there is a great chance we are making an overgeneralization.

Fallacy of Fairness

In this kind of thinking, we feel that life should be fair. Further, fairness should be according to our idea of it.

Now, when events do not match up to our notion of what is just, we become resentful.

People who fall prey to such frustration forget that their notion of fairness could be inaccurate. Alternatively, their evaluation of the situation could be fallacious. Or both. Instead, they conclude they have not been fairly treated, and hence, they are entitled to feel bitter.

Suppose, for example, Seema comes to know that Meena, her high performing friend, has been promoted. She concludes, 'They promoted Meena and overlooked me! That is not fair.'

Expecting a Catastrophe

In this distortion of reality, we expect the worst to happen. We hear of a problem and then imagine the worst for ourselves. For example, one hears of a theft in the neighbourhood and concludes, 'My home will also certainly be burgled.'

Likewise, a woman was informed that her neighbour's child had died in a car accident. She concluded, 'My god! My child drives through downtown to get to work. He will also have an accident.' In such thinking, an episode has been blown out of proportion. And then projected on to oneself.

Filtering out the Positives

In this thought process, we take negative details of a situation and make mountains out of them, while forgetting all the positive aspects. Here is an example.

One devotee called me and said, 'Swamiji, I am the most unfortunate man in the world. I am contemplating suicide.'

I said to him, 'Why are you so dejected? Think of the graces you have received.'

'What graces?' he replied. 'God has bestowed His graces on others and left none for me.'

'Okay, stay on the line,' I requested him, 'We will make a balance sheet of your blessings and miseries.'

'Swamiji, I have no blessings. So, you may as well cancel that column,' he said, pressing his point.

Ignoring his whining, I announced in a matter-of-fact tone, 'I am so sorry to learn that your wife ran away with another man and filed for a divorce against you.'

'What! Who told you that? My wife is very much at home and loves me dearly.'

'All right then. Let us write "loving wife" in the blessings column.'

Again, I said to him, 'I regret to hear that your children have been declared drug addicts and expelled from college.'

'Where did you get that from?' he exclaimed. 'My children are in professional colleges and excelling in academics.'

'Well then, let us note another grace of God, "good and responsible children".'

Next, I continued, 'I was saddened to know that your home was foreclosed by the bank.'

By now, he had caught on and began playing along. Together, we remembered the graces in his life. Finally, he concluded, 'Thank you for this eye-opening session. I had forgotten how blessed I am.'

The fact of the matter was that he did have many blessings but had been thinking only about the negatives in his life. It was a typical case of filtering where we single out an unpleasant detail and dwell on it exclusively. This creates a darkened vision of reality.

Imagined Mind Reading

This is the kind of thought process where we are sure we know what another person is thinking. And typically, we assume it is something negative about us.

For example, I am speaking to someone, and that person is not attentive. So, I assume that 'he does not like me'. In actuality, he may just have been distracted by some other important matter, but I have created a belief that has no foundation.

It could go even further, 'he hates me'.

Labelling

How many times have we fallen prey to this one! We observe a particular behaviour by a person and apply a tag: 'He is a jerk!', 'She is stupid!' and so on.

Additionally, the label we give is often emotionally loaded as 'ugly', 'cruel', 'careless' and the like.

We tag others in this manner and we tag ourselves too! We forget that all beings are eternal parts of the Supreme Divinity, who has blessed them with infinite potential for greatness. It is not for us to judge anyone. The Bible rightly states: 'Judge not, lest you be judged.' (Matthew 7.1)

Personalization

In this thought process, we assume personal blame for things that are outside our control. For example, one may say:

–   'My daughter married outside my religion. It is all my fault.'

- 'My son does not believe in God. I am a bad parent.'

Once we have erroneously usurped blame for something, we then begin repeating the thought in our mind until it bleeds deep into the consciousness.

Blaming

This is the reverse of personalization. People who engage in blaming others think that they are responsible for their emotional pain. Some examples of this are:

- 'You make me feel bad about myself.'

- 'Because of you, I feel discouraged.'

In reality, nobody can force us to feel in a particular way. But we have incorrectly blamed others for our negativity because it is easier than introspecting to find our weaknesses.

Imperative Thinking

In this disposition, we set the bar high and then project our expectations on others. And when people do not match up to our high expectations, we detest them for it.

The tendency here is to think in terms of 'should' and 'must', 'should not', and 'must not'. For instance:

- 'My neighbour "should" keep the front of his house perfectly clean.'

– 'My spouse "must" remember my birthday and take me out for dinner on that day.'

Likewise:

– 'My son "should not" think of anything apart from studies.'

– 'My daughter "should not" adopt a modern lifestyle.'

Here, the 'should' and 'must' statements have become a list of ironclad rules about how others need to behave. Similarly, some people apply such statements to themselves.

– I 'should not' have any desire for social media.

Now, when they are unable to match up to such statements, the consequence is emotional guilt.

Polarized Thinking

This is all-or-none thinking based on the false assumption that we must be fully successful, otherwise we will be absolute failures. It often contains words like 'never', 'every' and 'always'. There is no middle ground in this type of thinking. Some instances of it are:

– 'I did not get an A in maths. I will never succeed in life.'

– 'I was not selected for promotion. Therefore, my career is doomed.'

This can also be called black-and-white thinking. People who engage in it see things in extremes, while forgetting that human beings and situations are not two-dimensional. They have many shades and aspects to them.

Emotional Reasoning

In this mode of thinking, people use the logic: 'I feel something is true, so it must be true.' Such thinking blots out rationality. Emotional thinkers have no doubt that their negative emotions reflect the way things actually are. Here are some typical examples:

- 'I feel my business partner is cheating me. So, he must be cheating me; there can be no doubt of it.'

- 'I feel this deal will not work out well. So, it can never succeed, despite all the facts they are showing me.'

Excessively sentimental people easily fall prey to it. They accord such importance to their feelings that all reasoning becomes irrelevant.

Finger Pointing

This thinking is filled with fault-finding. We blame others for all the bad things happening in our life.

- 'If it were not for them, I would surely have been wealthier and happier.'

In this disposition, we do not accept personal responsibility for where we are in life. And since we are busy pointing fingers at others, we do not try to improve ourselves.

These are the most common kinds of faulty thinking. Let us now look at the remedies.

Combating Negative Thoughts

Over the past four decades, as a spiritual teacher, I have coached tens of thousands of people with all kinds of erroneous thought patterns. I have seen where they get stuck, what their cobwebs are and what solutions work for them. So, referring to our Vedic scriptures, modern science and personal experience, here are some tools to free ourselves from negative thinking.

Recognize the Thought

A million thoughts pass through the mind and make no difference to our life. It is safe to say, pernicious thoughts are not a problem in themselves; they are merely a mild nuisance. It is when we choose to believe them, by treating them as unassailable facts, that they get empowered. Thus, it is the power we give to them that traps us in their iron grip.

The first step, then, is to pause and recognize harmful thoughts when they arise. Here is how you can identify negative thoughts:

- Automatic: They pop into your mind without any effort from your side.

- Distorted: They do not connect with all the facts. They jump to conclusions.

- Unproductive: They undermine your motivation, feed bitterness and rob your optimism.

- Justifications: They provide excuses for you to be less than your best.

- Intrusive: They are disturbing or even vicious, and yet quite difficult to switch off.

To recognize the thoughts, so you can 'call out the critters', practise being more self-aware. You will discover that the moment you are aware of your negative thoughts, they lose their hold on you.

Challenge the Basis of the Thought

After identifying the critters, so to say, ask yourself, 'Is what I am believing really true?' If it is a mere assumption, think of evidence to the contrary. For example, if the mind says, 'Nobody likes me in the whole world,' remind yourself of the people who do love and care for you.

Then, label your compulsive thought pattern. Tag it as 'polarized thinking' or 'imperative thinking' or whatever it is. By labelling the thought pattern, you will diminish it.

Avoid Thought-Stopping

The Vedas inform us that suppression of thoughts does not work. Because they are not physical objects. Getting rid of an object is easy—pick it up from your room and place it elsewhere. But thoughts do not behave like that. They conduct themselves like little children. The more you tell kids not to do something, the more they wish to do it.

Suppose I tell you, 'Do not think of chocolate ice-cream in a crispy cone with caramel flowing down the sides. Do not visualize almond titbits embedded in it. You must absolutely not think of the plate by its side, containing potato chips with tomato ketchup. Don't even imagine a vegetable sandwich with lettuce and cheese.'

What will happen? Will you stop such thoughts on hearing my request? Or will they impinge more upon your mind?

Modern research studies confirm what Vedic texts declared thousands of years ago that suppressing thoughts has reverse effects. Recently, Amelia Aldao and Susan Nolen-Hoeksema, research psychologists from Yale, verified that strategies for suppression only increase anxiety.[2]

So, what should we do?

---

[2] Amelia Aldao and Susan Nolen-Hoeksema, 'Specificity of Cognitive Emotion Regulation Strategies: A Transdiagnostic Examination', NIH National Library of Medicine, 12 June 2010, https://pubmed.ncbi.nlm.nih.gov/20591413/

The Three-Step System

Dilution—Distance Yourself from the Thought

Have you noticed that you do not give the same amount of attention and weightage to all thoughts? 'Dilution' means reducing your attention to a negative thought.

Let us say you are walking on a lonely street and are confronted by an assailant. Ignoring him is not a good idea. Instead, you must consider either putting up a fight or running way.

But suppose children in your neighbourhood are heckling you. Now, confronting them or running away from them will not work. They will relish it and grow even more troublesome. Your best option will be to ignore them. When they realize they cannot disturb your peace, they will stop trying to irritate you.

Likewise, instead of fighting with a thought, 'Why did you come to my mind?' we dilute its impact. Treat the negative thought, not like an assailant, but as a little child. Every time a negative thought pops into your head, do not curse yourself, 'Why did I start thinking in this manner?' Else, the thought will become more virulent.

Instead, tell yourself, 'Let the mind indulge in its mischief. I will not associate with this emotion.' Like a snake whose venom has been removed, the thought will become innocuous.

This does not mean you justify your negative thinking or condone it. Just do not get upset about it. Maharshi Patanjali describes it thus:

abhyāsavairāgyābhyāṁ tannirodhaḥ   (sutra 1.12)

'Practising detachment from thoughts is the means for controlling the perturbations of the mind.' This has been explained in the previous chapter, in the section '*Sākṣī Bhav*—Watch Your Thoughts'.

Substitution—Replace a Negative Thought with a Positive Thought

Elimination of negative thoughts—when practised by itself—is difficult. It requires a mastery of mind management that most people do not possess. Instead, the easy way is to substitute the pernicious thought with a beneficial one.

If a negative thought is disturbing you, try to focus your mind on an opposite positive thought. The idea is to switch the harmful with the advantageous. This is called *pratipakṣha bhāvanā*. Maharshi Patanjali explains:

vitarkabādhane pratipakṣhabhāvanam   (sutra 2.33)

'When unwholesome thoughts contrary to self-discipline and goodness arise in the mind, the reverse thoughts should be practised.'

Pratipakṣha bhāvanā replaces the mind's focus from the negative to the positive, from bad thoughts to good ones, from harmful notions to beneficial ones.

For example, if thoughts of anger arise in the mind, think of love and patience; the positive thoughts do not necessarily have to be towards the same person with whom you are angry. The important thing is for the emotions to be positive, no matter where they are directed.

After the first two steps, the third one will clinch it.

Sublimation—Build a Positive Thought-Stream

Having turned your attention to positive emotions, now focus on building the thought chain further. Cultivate in your mind wholesome ideas of inspiration, optimism, cheerfulness, etc.

Or you can go a step further and consecrate your thoughts in the direction of the Supreme. Devotional sentiments are exceedingly powerful and can vanquish negative ones, like the light vanquishes darkness. Maharshi Patanjali recommends nurturing devotion as a technique for achieving mastery over the mind:

> *vishayavatī vā pravṛittirutpannā*
> *manasaḥ sthitinibandhinī*

> (*Yog Darshan* sutra 1.35)

'Steadiness of mind may be maintained by contemplating upon and becoming absorbed in God.'

The three-step formula given above is an internal practice. It is greatly aided by external support.

Associate with Positive People

A business simulation experiment was conducted by dividing employees into two groups. The groups were asked to finalize the distribution of bonuses to employees from an amount allocated for this purpose.

Unknown to the members, each group had one 'plant'. These were actors who had been secretly assigned to inject a trend of comments into the discussion. One was asked to inject optimistic and cheerful views. The other was asked to inject pessimistic thoughts into the conversation.

On the conclusion of their meeting, the first group felt good about their efforts. The second felt downbeat, without realizing why.

The conclusion was that negativity is contagious. But more importantly, positivity is also contagious. That is why the Ramayan recommends 'satsang', which means 'associating with holy personalities'. Satsang uplifts us with divine insights and sacred positivity. The Ramayan praises the power of satsang:

binu satasaṅg vivek na hoī,
  rām kṛipā binu sulabh na soī

This verse states that satsang helps us develop the ability to discern good thoughts from bad ones. It is by the infinite grace of Lord Ram that one gets the satsang of holy personalities.

4

Discipline Your Thoughts

O*n my morning walks in the US, I get to see a variety of dogs being walked by their owners. A few are well-trained and as they tread, they look neither left nor right. They have learnt to discipline themselves and shut out distractions.*

Most dogs, however, are extremely fidgety. One moment, a squirrel climbing up a tree grabs their attention. The next moment, they are sniffing an insect on the ground. The very next, they turn their gaze to a woman walking by and then a man. The poor dog walker holding the leash is constantly yanked to the left and the right on the pathway.

Our mind behaves in a similar manner. It vacillates between hankering and aversion, love and hatred. But behind it is the urge of our lower nature propelling us in the direction of maximum pleasure.

The Pleasure Principle

We had compared our mind to a little child. A toddler does not care for long-term benefits; it pursues pleasure in the moment. Our mind has the same nature. It is primarily motivated by the urge for pleasure. It seeks a variety of gratifications for enjoyment, such as fame, power and love.

This proclivity, also known as the pleasure principle, forms the lower nature in us humans. It hankers for the delights of the senses. It seeks satisfaction from comfort and luxury. The problem is that enjoying these carnal pleasures is akin to the proverbial elephant's bath. The elephant bathes in a stream and after emerging from the water, it takes the mud from the riverbank and sprays it on itself.

The same is the case with our yearnings for glamour, glitter and gratification. We can compare them to an itch. Hoping to get relief, we scratch the itch, but doing so only aggravates the problem. The itch comes back and it's even more irksome; it can even heighten to a sore. But if we tolerate it, it first causes discomfort and then subsides.

Compare this phenomenon to the 'Cobra Effect'.[1]

---

[1] Matthew Rolnick, 'Beware of the Cobra Effect in Business', Forbes, 26 August 2020, https://www.forbes.com/sites/forbesbusinessdevelopmentcouncil/2020/08/26/beware-of-the-cobra-effect-in-business/?sh=1c82a92c5f6f

During British rule in India, a phenomenon was observed that led to the name 'Cobra Effect'. The government had grown concerned about the number of venomous cobras in Delhi. It announced a bounty for every dead cobra that was deposited at the local government offices.

The incentive paid off initially as large numbers of cobras were killed. After a while, however, people turned it into a means of earning and began breeding cobras for money. This only served to increase the population of the venomous snake.

When the government caught on, it scrapped the reward scheme. Cobras being raised for business were now worthless. So, their owners set them free, which led to a further spike in the number of cobras.

Since then, the term 'Cobra Effect' has come to represent a cure for a problem that only aggravates it. The nature of desires is the same—attempts to quench them through momentary gratifications only heighten the problem.

Just as we seek pleasure, we also run from pain. When we perceive misery somewhere, our mind begins to contemplate it. Our mind, goaded by its nature, engages in contemplating pleasure and pain, again and again. It keeps shuttling between thoughts of hankering and aversion, and these change from one moment to the next. The Vedas call them *saṅkalp* (hankering) and *vikalp* (aversion).

Then what is the way to real happiness? It will become clear in the next section.

Difference between Pleasure and Happiness

Maximizing pleasure and minimizing pain is everyone's goal. We 'hope' it will make us happy. This is why we want tastier food and wine, softer beds, jazzier gadgets and so on. The multinational corporations sell us 'fun' in the guise of happiness. The terms 'Happy Meals' and 'Happy Hour' are popularly used in restaurants. Entertainment venues are all around, and catchy advertising seduces people to try new products and activities.

Yet, the deep abiding joy they seek eludes most people. Those who sell you a fancy phone, a new car or a bigger home might like you to believe that you can buy a lot of happiness with your money. But the truth is that money can only buy you fun or comfort; it cannot buy you happiness.

Let us understand the difference between the two. Pleasure results from enjoying external things like food, movies or games. It is a momentary feeling that remains while we savour these objects, but later it is gone. So, we have to procure those objects again to continue feeling the enjoyment. And then, again. And again. This quickly becomes a vicious cycle. Consequently, people get addicted to external stimulations. Then serious problems ensue.

Happiness, on the other hand, requires nothing from the outside. You do not need to go around the world to find it. **True happiness is experienced as a consequence of who you are. It is a state of inner joy that comes from living up to your ideals; a sense of fulfilment on doing something worthwhile.** It is consistently stable—not ephemeral—and remains with us day and night. The more we savour it, the better we feel.

Guru Nanak was a bhakti saint who lived in Punjab in medieval times. An episode from his life illustrates this difference. According to a popular folklore, he once visited the court of the Mughal emperor, Babar. The king offered his guest, the saintly Nanak, a cup of bhang *(marijuana) and suggested that he savour it.*

Guru Nanak, who was experiencing the bliss of the divine Name of God that was always on his lips, responded:

> *bhāng tambākū chhutarā utar jāt prabhāt*
> *nām khumārī nānakā charhī rahe din rāt*

'O King! The inebriation of bhang and tobacco will be gone tomorrow morning. But the bliss of the divine Name that I am relishing remains with me day and night.'

The inner bliss which Guru Nanak talks about requires no intoxicants. In fact, it is independent of externals. Hence, there are people who go through great pain and adversity and yet are joyous. While external pleasures and material comforts are missing in their lives, inwardly, they are ever content and happy. Contrast them with people who are surrounded by luxury sedans, palatial homes and fashionable clothes, but have no joy within.

The Neurology of Pleasure versus Happiness

Neurologically, the experience of pleasure involves the stimulation of our brain's reward system through the release of dopamine—the excitatory neurotransmitter that always promises but never fulfils. Corporations catering to our consumer-driven society keep finding newer ways of stimulating dopamine in our brain.

Satya Nadella, the CEO of Microsoft, recommended a book to all his associates—*Hooked: How to Build Habit-Forming Products*.[2] Its popularity was not limited to Microsoft. The marketing departments of Apple, Google, PayPal and Amazon made it their Bible. It ranked as the number one bestseller in the

---

[2] Nir Eyal with Julie Li, *Indistractable: How to Control Your Attention and Choose Your Life*, Bloomsbury, January 2020, Introduction, Kindle

Wall Street Journal and the number one book in the 'Products' category on Amazon. These companies knew that to sell their product, they needed customers to keep coming back for more. Their business model depended upon it.

However, since we are customers, not sellers, we are at the receiving end. We must bear in mind that the more a product gives us a dopamine rush, the more addictive it is. There is momentary gratification, followed by regret. Consequently, the more pleasure we seek, the unhappier we become. This applies to all the delights of the senses and pleasures of the flesh.

On the other hand, the experience of happiness is very different from pleasure. Physiologically, it is attributed not to dopamine, but to another brain chemical called serotonin. This is not an excitatory chemical but a pacifying one. Serotonin does not fire the neurons. Rather, it calms them down. So, it does not work up a torturous thirst. Instead, it bestows inner fulfilment. It can never be addictive, and hence, you never hear of someone being hurt by an overdose of inner joy.

Such joy is fulfilling, but achieving it requires discipline and hard work. It is unlike pleasures that are experienced from sense objects. If we wish to relish real happiness, we must stop being slaves of our mind and senses. Let us discuss this next.

Freedom Comes from Discipline

Freedom is a hugely misunderstood concept. Many people consider the unbridled opportunity for fun and pleasure as their idea of freedom. They dislike control, and instead, choose a lifestyle of wanton actions and unfettered attitudes. They do not realize that while shunning external regulations, they unwittingly remain servants of their own mind. They end up becoming like slot machines, whose behaviour is controlled by the buttons of their senses. Freedom is a huge misnomer in describing such a situation.

What, then, is true freedom? It is the strength to stop getting knocked by our biological conditioning. Only that person can really claim to be free who has learnt to resist the urges of the lower nature. That is why, the Bhagavad Gita states:

> *rāga-dveṣha-viyuktais tu*
> * viṣhayān indriyaiśh charan*
> *ātma-vaśhyair-vidheyātmā*
> * prasādam adhigachhhati*   (verse 2.64)

'One who controls the mind, and is free from attachment and aversion, relishes divine bliss even while using the objects of the senses.'

The liberty to live to our life's fullest potential comes not from indulgence, but steely discipline. Only by subduing our lower instincts can we lift ourselves up. Compare this to the kite that flies high in the air.

The festival of Makar Sankranti is celebrated around 14 January every year. In many places in India, people mark the day by flying kites.

During one such Makar Sankranti celebration, a father was giving his five-year-old son his first lesson in kite-flying. 'Son, what is keeping the kite up?' he asked.

'Father, it is the strong wind that is blowing,' replied the boy.

'No, my child. It is the string tied to it.'

'But father, the string is pulling it down.'

'Okay,' said the father. 'Release the string and see what happens.'

The moment the child released the string, the kite began gliding and slowly descended to the ground. 'See,' said the father, 'it seems paradoxical, but the kite was flying high because the string pulling it was taut.'

Like the taut string allowing the kite to fly high, **discipline enables us to do what we want in life because it liberates us from the slavery of our mind.** Hence, for any worthwhile accomplishment, we must learn to break free from the grip of the mind and senses.

– Our senses may yearn for sweets and fried foods, but if we wish to remain healthy, we must learn to deny them.

– The body may complain when we exercise, but we must bear the discomfort if we wish to keep ill-health at bay.

– Our mind may prefer the joy of an extended weekend, but we must reject it if we hope to be selected for the forthcoming promotion in the office.

– Our ego may hate to apologize, but we must refuse to give in to it if we wish to save the relationship.

Self-discipline is the mental power that enables us to stick to our plans. It stops us from changing our mind, even when the situation is unpleasant. With self-discipline, we can lose weight, study harder and work more. We can control our speech, correct our behaviour and run marathons.

Without self-control, we fall prey to every alluring distraction in the environment. We become victims of the slightest temptation for gratification. And we are vulnerable to the trap of vices and addictions.

It is the virtue of self-restraint that allows us to persevere in the face of difficulties. When laziness and carelessness attack us, it is self-discipline that comes to our rescue. It empowers us to break old habits and establish new ones. Equipped with it, we can get things done with a commitment to excellence. No wonder that discipline is called the 'king of virtues'.

Do the Opposite of the Mind's Urges

Both pleasant and unpleasant situations will come our way as long as we live. That is the nature of the world. What we need is to learn to tolerate them. The Bhagavad Gita states:

> *mātrā-sparśhās tu kaunteya*
> *   śhītoṣhṇa-sukha-duḥkha-dāḥ*
> *āgamāpāyino 'nityās*
> *   tans-titikṣhasva bhārata*   (verse 2.14)

'O Arjun! The fleeting perceptions of happiness and distress arise because of contact between the senses and the sense objects. These come and go like the winter and summer seasons. Remember, they are not permanent. Hence, endure them without being disturbed.'

This beautiful verse from the Bhagavad Gita provides us the secret to free ourselves from serfdom to our mind. Tolerance is the key to subduing the mind. Every time our mind asks us to do something that is not beneficial to our higher purpose, rather than succumbing to it, tolerate the urge.

Suppose the mind suggests, 'Let me surf the Internet for entertainment.' We know it will serve no purpose and be a complete waste of time. Yet, so often, we give in to the urge and indulge in the fun. This strengthens the mind, and it holds greater sway over us the next time.

Instead, we can stand up to the urge and say, 'No, killing time is pointless; surfing the Internet will do me no good. My dear mind, I will not listen to you.' By refusing to gratify the desire for pleasure, we loosen the grip of the mind over us. The more we repeat such behaviour, the more our mind gets subdued.

Every time we resist the urge for momentary gratification, we break the mind's control over us. Conversely, each time we indulge in an inferior pleasure against the wisdom of our intellect, the mind tightens its hold on us. Therefore, refuse to capitulate to your mind, and it will develop respect for you.

The Dhammapada states emphatically:

Humans are caught in the strands of desire and attachment; they are stuck like spiders in their own web. The wise cut these bonds asunder and free themselves of all their suffering, without looking back.

(verse 24:14)

Jagadguru Kripaluji Maharaj states in his composition, *Sadhana Karu Pyare*:

man ko māno śhatru usakī,
  sunahu jani kachhu pyāre (verse 43)

'Dear one! See the mind as your enemy. Do not listen to anything it says.' The reason for our conditioning is we have allowed the mind the freedom to dictate terms to us. Now we must reverse it. The idea is to break the conditioning created by the pleasure principle.

Rise above the Mind's Likes and Dislikes

Apart from sensual delights, the material mind gets gratification in many other ways. It loves gossiping about others and engaging in futile character assassination. Statistics reveal that fifty per cent of the conversation in offices is about others. If it was about their achievements, it may have been inspirational. Invariably, however, it is about people's weaknesses and shortcomings.

Why do we love fault-finding? Because it gratifies the ego and tastes like sweet nectar to the material mind. 'If the other person is bad, then I need not feel guilty about not being good myself.'

To become the master of your mind, you must desist from fault-finding, no matter how pleasant it seems. Jagadguru Kripaluji Maharaj states in *Sadhana Karu Pyare*:

> *lakhahuñ jani paradoṣh kabahuñ,*
> *doṣh nij lakhu pyāre*   (verse 22)

'Dear one! Never look at the faults of others; turn your attention to your own shortcomings.' These are the simple disciplines that set us free.

Likewise, our mind hates to hear criticism about ourselves. The moment someone chides us, we recoil, and when we are praised, we feel elated. Forcing ourselves to do the reverse kills the grip of our ego. Along these lines, Saint Kabir states:

niṅdak niyare rākhiye, āñgan kuṭi chhabāy
bin sābun pānī binā, nirmal kare subhāy

'If you are sincere about disciplining your mind, find those who criticize you. Allow them the freedom to vent themselves, while you simply tolerate. You will discover that, without any effort, your mind will be cleansed.'

Now let us extend the principle of tolerance further. Our mind has its set of likes and dislikes, which make us happy or sad. However, these very thoughts keep us fettered in their groove. Based on them, we indulge in hankering and aversion. To unfetter ourselves, we must go beyond these puny likes and dislikes, and focus on our higher purpose.

Pushpa and Meena were colleagues, and their cubicles were adjacent to each other. They were the best of friends but also the worst of enemies.

Meena had a way of doing things that Pushpa could just not come to terms with. No matter what she did, it *would get Pushpa thinking, 'If only she would act **this** way instead of **that** way, I would be much happier and more productive.'*

This cycle would repeat itself daily, and sometimes even hourly. Then one day, Pushpa realized her own likes and dislikes were the cause of her problems. She needed Meena to behave in a certain way because her own mind was familiar with it, and that would make her feel comfortable.

Pushpa understood that Meena was not the problem, rather, her own mind was the issue. She decided to adopt a different way of thinking. Every time Meena did something, Pushpa gave her the benefit of the doubt and tried to view the situation from her colleague's perspective. 'What would I do if I were in her shoes?' Such thoughts changed the equation. Now she no longer needed Meena to change. She had learnt to resist the dictates of her own mind.

The techniques discussed in this chapter will empower our intellect to subdue the mind. By denying it the liberty of likes and dislikes, we will develop a measure of dispassion. Now, let us take it a step further in demolishing unprofitable thought patterns.

5

How Thoughts Are Created

In science, there is a raging debate about the nature of thoughts. Do they fall in the category of electromechanical energy? Or are they a different form of energy, beyond the present reach of science? A similar controversy exists about the origin of thoughts. Are they created by the brain? Or is there a separate entity called the mind which is distinct from the brain?

Please be warned that this chapter is going to get very technical and scientific. If you relish a blend of philosophy and science, then do proceed with it. However, if philosophical dialectics does not interest you and you are simply reading this book for practical wisdom, then do not hesitate to skip this chapter.

Nature of Thoughts

Scientists are divided in their opinion on the nature of thoughts, feelings, ideas and perceptions. The more popular theory states that thoughts are created by chemical reactions in the brain. It explains thus:

When we are exposed to external stimuli, they cause electric impulses in our brain. These impulses travel like waves along the axons, which connect the neurons together. As a signal reaches the end of an axon, it causes the release of chemical neurotransmitters into a corresponding synapse. The synapse is a chemical junction point between the axon tip and the target neuron. The target neuron then responds with its own electric signal, which spreads to other neurons. Like a chain reaction, the electric signal spreads to billions of neurons, causing corresponding chemical reactions in a few milliseconds. The kind of thought generated is determined by the nature of the neurons that were fired and the chemical reactions that were triggered.

This prevailing understanding of science is very reductionist. It assumes thoughts to be nothing more than physical and chemical energy. It does not answer questions like: 'How do the chemical reactions in the brain create beliefs, values and purpose?

Further, electrochemical phenomena can be replicated by machines. If thoughts are just chemical reactions, then technically we should be able to create machines that feel and imagine. 'It is a tall order,' writes Evelina Fedorenko, associate professor and laboratory head in the Brain and Cognitive Sciences department at MIT,[1] implying that such a simplistic understanding of thoughts leaves a huge portion of the human experience unexplained.

Look at it another way. If we expend physical or chemical energy, it decreases. But if we utilize our knowledge, it increases. It means knowledge residing in our intellect is not a gross energy. Rather, our thoughts, opinions and ideas are manifestations of a metaphysical energy.

Difference between Mind and Brain

We often use the words brain and mind interchangeably. But are they both the same thing? We compliment a person for having a terrific mind. We wonder what is going on in another's mind. We even say someone is out of his mind. But when the question arises, 'What is the mind?', scientists realize that defining it is a surprisingly slippery task.

Again, the majority of scientists have taken a reductionist viewpoint. They theorize that the mind is a product of the brain's activity. They claim that the brain's neurons get fired to create perceptions, and the mind is nothing but the sum total of these perceptions.

---

[1] Elizabeth Dougherty, 'What are Thoughts Made Of?', MIT School of Engineering, 26 April 2011, https://engineering.mit.edu/engage/ask-an-engineer/what-are-thoughts-made-of/

As research progresses, however, evidence continues to accumulate against this simplistic viewpoint. There are cases where someone's brain gets damaged, and yet, the mind continues to function normally; the ability to think remains unaffected. Even more interesting are cases where the brain's two hemispheres are separated by surgery.

Roger Sperry won the Nobel Prize in physiology or medicine in 1981. He studied the outcome of the surgery called corpus callosotomy, which is also performed in some cases of severe epilepsy.[2]

The theory behind the procedure is that a seizure happening in one half of the brain is a minor seizure. But when it travels to the second half of the brain, it becomes a major seizure. Therefore, in corpus callosotomy, the brain is split into two. This prevents a seizure happening in one half from spreading and becoming a major one.

If the mind and the brain were the same and the brain was split into two, then two distinct people should have been created from one person. However, Roger Sperry's study revealed that the person remained one and not two. In fact, if you were to speak to such

---

[2] M.S. Gazzaniga, J. E. Bogen, and R. W. Sperry, 'Some Functional Effects of Sectioning the Cerebral Commissures in Man, PNAS, 1 October 1962, https://www.pnas.org/doi/full/10.1073/pnas.48.10.1765

people, they would seem normal; you would not realize that they possess two separate brains.

Imagine sawing a computer in half and then realizing that it is still functioning the same as before. This was such a colossal discovery regarding the human brain that Roger Sperry was awarded the Nobel prize for it. If splitting the brain does not majorly affect the mind, it proves that the mind and brain are not the same thing.

Again, take the case of plants. They have no brain, and yet they have a mind. J.C. Bose, an Indian scientist, was a leader in this area of research in the first part of the twentieth century. He used a crescograph, which he had invented, to measure plant response to various stimuli, thereby scientifically proving parallelism between animal and plant tissues. His experiments proved that even plants possess a mind. They perceive the moods of their gardener, and in response, they speed up or slow down their growth.

Like plants, flatworms also do not have a brain. Yet, they can perform 'intelligent' functions.

This implies that the mind's function extends far beyond the gross tangible workings of the brain's neurons. It encompasses the intangible, invisible and transcendent world of feelings, attitudes and beliefs.

If the brain and the mind were the same entity, then brain scans should have been able to read the mind. However, an experiment was conducted where the brain scans of people were given to seventy independent teams for analysis. They all reached completely dissimilar conclusions. The scientific study was published in the article, 'Variability in the Analysis of a Single Neuroimaging Dataset by Many Teams', published in the journal *Nature* in its May 2020 issue.

In conclusion, the brain and mind are different. The brain is a localized physical organ situated in the head. The mind, however, is not restricted to the head. According to the Vedic scriptures, it resides in the region of our heart and permeates every cell of our body. Hence, its tremendous power over all bodily systems.

In English literature, the mind is often referred to as the heart. The reason is that people intuitively realize the seat of the mind is in the heart region. That is why, in love and hate, the emotions are felt in the heart.

People thus say things like, 'Her heart was elsewhere', 'He did the work with all his heart', etc. In such expressions, the 'heart' does not mean the physical heart because it has no emotions. It refers to the mind. To avoid any confusion with the physical heart, we can call the mind the 'ethereal heart'.

How the Mind Uses the Brain

The mind employs the brain for its functioning. Compare it to the way a computer works. It has the hardware, which is the physical component, and the software, which runs on it and is virtual. Likewise, the brain is the hardware that the mind utilizes for running software-like programs of thoughts and feelings. Hence, thoughts and emotions lead to concomitant neural firings and synaptic chemical reactions.

But this does not mean that thoughts are merely neural firings and nothing further. When we think, electroencephalographs can pick up alpha, beta, gamma and theta waves that our brain emanates. So, some researchers erroneously jump to the conclusion that thoughts are merely the waves that are measured in electroencephalography but this assumption is way off the mark. It is like hearing the roar of a lion which is out of sight and concluding from it that the lion is nothing beyond sound energy since we cannot see it. Likewise, just because the electroencephalograph picks up alpha, beta and gamma waves from the brain, we cannot conclude that thoughts are nothing more than them. The fact is that thoughts—which are generated by the mind—are a subtle energy form.

In conclusion, thinking is an activity the mind performs by accessing the hardware of the brain. Thus, the mind is limited by the abilities of the brain to some extent.

It is pertinent to mention here that not all thoughts require the brain's intercession. There are varieties of thoughts that can be generated by the mind even without accessing the brain's hardware.

Does Enlightenment Require Thoughts?

Is enlightenment a thoughtless state? If not, are enlightened thoughts of the same nature as material thoughts? Many people express the curiosity to understand this. Hence, a detailed explanation is called for.

The Vedas explain that there are four kinds of *vāṇīs* (thought forms) that humans are capable of.

Parā Vāṇī

We have all experienced moments when an epiphany takes place—an understanding of a truth that was previously eluding us. This sudden deeper knowledge of a subject does not dawn upon us in words; it seems to happen in a moment, like the dispelling of darkness by the light.

One may ask, 'Does this kind of illumination of knowledge require words or thoughts?' The Vedas respond by explaining that it requires neither. This dawning of knowledge happens in *parā vāṇī*, or divine language, which is beyond thoughts. Similarly, the state of enlightenment is beyond words and thoughts.

Paśhyanti Vāṇī

Parā vāṇī is a process of knowledge that does not utilize thoughts. In *paśhyanti vāṇī,* we do think, but without the use of words.

We all have experience of this one as well. Every so often, thoughts and feelings just happen to us. We process them in words much later. Such thinking is *paśhyanti vāṇī.*

Madhyamā Vāṇī

In this type of *vāṇī*, we think with the help of words. It is a far slower form of thinking.

Evolved souls laugh at us when they see us engage in this gross form of thinking. But it is a fact that we do use *madhyamā vāṇī* as well, while thinking.

Vaikharī Vāṇī

These are the thoughts that are accompanied by concurrent spoken words. It is possible that, alongside *vaikharī vāṇī*, one may engage in other forms of thinking as well.

I do hope that after reading about the different kinds of thinking, you would have realized that thoughts are far more than the electro-chemical reactions happening in the brain. They are subtle energy forms created by the mind, with or without the assistance of the brain.

With that knowledge, we can now go deeper into how neural wirings in the brain create highways for thoughts.

6

Neural Highways and Thought Structures

If wild grass grows in your rose garden, it is persistent. You cut the grass and it grows back. The permanent solution is to weed it out from the root. In the same fashion, pernicious patterns of thought arise from an original cause that is not directly obvious. Without addressing that source, all attempts at eradication remain superficial. What, then, is the root of negative thoughts?

The following story provides a hint.

A professor was with his students after his class. They were gathered in a corridor between the classrooms. The professor held a cup of coffee in one hand and was answering questions being posed to him.

Another group of students came walking down the walkway, deeply engrossed in conversation. One of them accidentally bumped into the professor, jolting the coffee cup in his hand and spilling the coffee on the floor.

The professor was nonchalant. Instead of getting angry, he asked the students, with admirable calmness, 'Why do you think the coffee spilled on the floor?'

'Your hand was jutting out from your body,' volunteered one student.

'We were gathered in the wrong place,' said another.

'You weren't holding the cup firmly enough,' a third student suggested.

'Wrong!' replied the professor. 'The reason why the coffee spilled on the floor was because the cup was full. Had it been filled with tea, it would have spilled on the floor too.'

Similarly, the reason our mind generates fetid thoughts is that it is contaminated. Had it been brimming with goodness, it would have created thoughts of a similar nature. The plain principle is that a pure mind creates empowering thoughts, while an impure mind produces weakening thoughts.

This leads us to the next question. Why is our mind impure?

The Impure Mind

If I were to gather a bin full of stinky garbage and dump it on the Kashmiri carpet in your living room, how would you react? Taking it a step further, if I were to gather a bucketful of vermin from a drain and let them loose in your bedroom, what would you do? It is likely that you would pull a revolver on me and say, 'Clean this up!' Alternatively, you would call the police.

We all like keeping our home and environment clean. Even trash that we produce is repulsive to us, and we keep it out of sight and smell. When we cannot tolerate dirt in our home, is it not astonishing that we do not hesitate to load our mind with filth in the form of anger, greed, hatred and envy? Why such a self-indicting pursuit?

The reason for it is *rāg* (attachment) and *dveṣh* (hatred). They cause the object of attachment or hatred to repeatedly come to our mind and dirty it. Consider the following episode.

Hari Makhijani sold his factory because his children were not interested in continuing the manufacturing line of their business. A week after the sale was complete, the factory caught fire. Seeing it burn, Hari Makhijani began weeping at the loss.

'Father, what are you weeping for?' asked his son. 'Have you forgotten that we sold the factory seven days ago?'

On hearing this, Hari Makhijani relaxed. Poor fellow! He had sold the factory, but the residual attachment to it was still pillaging his head.

When the mind is attached, the object of attachment clings to it. Its thoughts repeatedly come to the mind, disturbing its calm. Now, if the attachment were to God, we would be deluged by godly thoughts, and these would have purified our mind. However, we are attached to material entities in the realm of the three gunas (three modes of nature—goodness, passion and ignorance) which are impure. Consequently, our mind too is tainted by their thoughts.

To cleanse our mind, we will have to eliminate *rāg* and *dvesh*. So, let us see how these two develop and what is the way of demolishing them.

What Causes Attachment?

The reason why the mind gets attached is perfectly explained in the Bhagavad Gita, with clarity and preciseness.

dhyāyato vishayān punsah sangas teshūpajāyate

(verse 2.62)

'While contemplating the objects of the senses, one develops attachment to them.'

When we repeatedly think there is happiness somewhere, our mind becomes appended to that object. In Vedic terminology, it is called *āsakti*, which is the clinging of our mind to an object. Take the case of attachment to comfort foods, such as chai or coffee.

Most Indians will never refuse a cup of chai. It seems to comfort the senses and relax the mind. But this habit of drinking tea was not indigenous.

My grandparents would often tell me that during colonial rule, the British had established vast tea gardens in the country for export of the produce to England. Consumption of the drink in India was largely unknown. However, tea garden owners shrewdly transplanted the habit in the local populace.

A tea truck would visit a neighbourhood and offer a free cup to whoever cared for it. Slowly, a cost of 1 paisa started getting extracted for a cup. Then the rate was doubled to 2 paise. And then 5 paise.

As people kept drinking, the clasp of chai on people's mind grew stronger. Today, if you wish to purchase a cup of tea at the railway station, it will cost you Rs 10.

Vast segments of the population are now attached to tea. How did this happen? When they savoured the first cup, it gave a tiny bit of pleasure to the palate. The nicotine content also made the brain feel slightly lighter. People started contemplating happiness in that experience. 'Tea will give pleasure . . . tea will give pleasure . . .' The recurrence of this thought with every cup drunk led to attachment to chai.

Ask a tea addict, 'This concoction does not have either proteins or vitamins. Why do you drink it?'

The person will reply, 'If I do not consume tea, I feel dizzy. When I drink a cup, my head feels normal.'

The mind has now developed 'love' for chai. And what led to it? The person's own repeated thoughts, 'There is happiness in chai'.

The brain assists the mind in creating attachment. The recurrence of thought triggers the synaptic plasticity of the brain and changes its neural configuration. It creates an expressway of neurons to facilitate those thoughts. You may have noticed that **if you are attached to someone, his or her thoughts repeatedly come to your mind. That is because the brain has created neural highways for facilitating thoughts of that person.**

What Causes Hatred?

Hate is compulsive attachment to a set of negative memories and the emotions they evoke. Like love, hate can be an all-consuming passion. It is a form of neurosis, wherein the mind gets fixated and judgement gets altered.

Harbouring hatred for an extended duration devastates both body and mind. It even alters the brain's chemistry by triggering the 'fight or flight response'. This increases the secretion of cortisol and adrenaline. Hence, it contributes to insomnia, weight gain and depression. Paranoia, restlessness and bitterness are all side-effects of hatred.

I once counselled a person who was estranged from his brother. They had not talked in years. While he recalled how his brother had wronged him, his anger kept mounting. Finally, it breached all limits and he exclaimed, 'See what he has done to me!'

I let a few moments go by until he was calm enough to listen. Then I responded, 'See what you have done to yourself. Have you been wronged? Yes, but you have taken one bad experience and churned it in your head until it has burnt you physically and emotionally.'

Life is a continual series of problems and difficulties, and disappointments are unavoidable. Harbouring compulsive thoughts of bitterness does not help the situation in any way. Instead, obsessive negativity hurts the hater himself.

The problem is that such thoughts are bittersweet. They inflate the ego in a self-righteous way. They make the hater feel superior and relish resentment in a tamasic (of the mode of ignorance) way.

The objects of hatred can be many. The target of animosity could be the boss at office who treated us badly. Or bitterness could be towards a loved one who betrayed us, like an ex-spouse. Else, hatred could manifest for the one we feel threatened by, as in the case of racial hatred. People of one race fear the other race will harm their self-interest.

Dr Brian Weiss is an American psychiatrist and hypnotherapist who specializes in past-life regression. He is the author of the bestselling, Many Lives, Many Masters.

Born in a traditional Jewish family, he initially did not believe in reincarnation. However, as a traditional psychotherapist, Dr Weiss was astonished when one of his young patients, Catherine, began recalling past-life traumas. His scepticism eroded when, under hypnotherapy, Catherine related incidents from previous past lifetimes that he could publicly verify. Apparently, in one of their past lives, Catherine and Dr Weiss were connected as well.[1]

This completely changed his perspective. Dr Weiss successfully conducted past-life regression on thousands of people and wrote many books. He can be credited for popularizing belief in reincarnation of the soul in the Western world.

In his book, Same Soul, Many Bodies, *Dr Weiss writes that based on his experience having regressed*

---

[1] Adapted from Dr Brian Weiss, *Many Lives, Many Masters*, Simon & Schuster, Kindle

thousands of patients to their past lives, 'the surest way to be reincarnated into a particular group of people, defined by religion, race, nationality, or culture is to hate those people in a previous life, to be prejudiced or violent against that group.'[2]

That is so interesting. By hating a particular religion, the soul took birth in that very religion in its next birth. God says, 'You are not supposed to hate anyone. Until you learn to stop loathing, you cannot evolve to higher levels. So, if you bitterly despise something, I will arrange for you to overcome that animosity in your next life.' It is, therefore, of paramount importance to get out of the vicious trap of hatred.

Now let us come to the crucial question: Why does hatred develop? The answer is that hate develops just as attachment does. When we repeatedly ruminate, 'This object gives me misery, this object is harmful to me,' the chain of negative musings solidifies the bitterness.

Again, let us see how the brain cooperates with the mind in creating hatred. Repetition of thought causes synaptic plasticity to kick in, and the consequence is neural learning in the direction of negativity. Networks develop in the brain to facilitate future repetition of

---

[2] Dr Brain Weiss, *Same Soul, Many Bodies*, Simon & Schuster, 2004, Chapter 3, Kindle

the particular negative idea. Consequently, the bitter thought impinges frequently upon our mind, and the state of loathing achieves perpetuity.

We have discussed two types of emotions: attachment and hatred. The Vedas look on them both as identical states. The *Patanjali Yog Sutras* state:

sukhānuśhayī rāgaḥ
duḥkhānuśhayī dveṣhaḥ (*Sadhana Pada* 7–8)

'Contemplation of pleasure results in attachment, while contemplation of suffering results in aversion.'

While attachment is affection in a positive sense, hatred is the same emotion in a negative sense. In both states, the mind becomes clasped. While in attachment, the object of our affection impinges on our mind, in hatred, images of the hated object overwhelm us.

The problem is that attachment is only the beginning. From it, come wanting and craving. Let us see how the progression takes place.

Desires Put Us in the State of Wanting

The attached mind makes us think: 'This object will make me feel good; I need it.' It puts us into the 'state of wanting', which is what desire is. The Bhagavad Gita states:

saṅgāt sañjāyate kāmaḥ (verse 2.62)

'Attachment leads to desire.' A mother who is attached to her baby finds that thoughts of the baby flood her mind. Those attached to sweets find thoughts of chocolates swamping their mind.

The specific desire you repeatedly experience is based on your attachment. If you wish to know where your mind is attached, you can introspect and see where your mind repeatedly runs when you are idle. If it runs to your family members, that is where your attachment is. If it runs to money, know it to be the object of your fondness.

If, instead, we wish to still our mind and free it from the trap of desire, we will need to give up attachment. It's as simple as that! We can learn from how monkeys get trapped.

It is well-known in Indian villages that monkey trainers have a very interesting way of trapping the animals. The trainer who wishes to catch wild monkeys selects a suitable spot in the jungle. There, he digs a hole in the ground and buries a long-necked bottle in it halfway, with its neck jutting out. He then fills half the bottle with peanuts and leaves.

A monkey arrives and discovers the bottle with the delicious peanuts. It looks around and confirms that no human being is around. To get at the peanuts, the monkey straightens its hand and inserts it into the bottle. It grabs a fistful of peanuts and then tries to extract its hand. However, its fist is larger than the bottle's neck and the monkey is unable to extract its hand. It screams and tugs but finally gives up. A while later, the trainer arrives, hits it unconscious and carries it away.

The poor monkey does not realize that it could have easily extracted its hand from the bottle by releasing the peanuts. It believes that it is trapped. Likewise, we may think that people or objects are to blame for snaring our mind, without realizing our own attachment is the cause.

Jalaluddin Rumi, the thirteenth-century Sufi saint, said it beautifully: 'Why do you stay in prison when the door is wide open?'[3] He was referring to the prison of attachment that binds our mind.

Having understood the science of desire through the scriptures, let me take you into the neurology of it. The topic is a bit complex but extremely interesting.

The Physiology of Desire

In chapter 5, 'How Thoughts Are Created', we discussed that the mind is like the software and the brain is its

---

[3] 'My New Favourite Poem – Rumi's "A Community of the Spirit"', The Line Break, 10 Jan 2013, https://thelinebreak.wordpress.com/2013/01/10/rumi-a-community-of-the-spirit/

hardware. The mind utilizes the brain in the thinking process. Hence, our thought patterns condition and configure the neural structures of the brain.

But the reverse is also true. The conditioned brain forces the mind to think particular thoughts. In this case, the object of attachment becomes the 'trigger'. Sight or thoughts of it prompt the creation of desire. For example, when we view sexually graphic material, it provokes the discharge of dopamine in the brain.

Dopamine is a brain chemical involved in the pursuit of happiness. Other important brain chemicals related to the feeling of happiness are serotonin, oxytocin and endorphin. However, dopamine is different from all of them. **Interestingly, dopamine does not make us feel happy. It merely creates an expectation of future happiness.** Thus, dopamine does not give satisfaction. Rather, it creates the 'hope' of satisfaction. 'Oh, I will get happiness here. I definitely need this.'

Although it is only a future promise, it hijacks the intellect. Simultaneously, a tension gets created: 'If I do not get this object, I will suffer the absence of happiness.'

Then, we create desire with the expectation of pleasure and release from tension. What is the nature of desire? It is the 'feeling of wanting'.

Now let us see what happens when we fulfil the desire.

How Craving Develops

The Ramayan states: *jimi pratilābh lobh adhikāī.* 'If you satisfy desire, it results in craving.' This is just as offering ghee into the fire does not diminish it but inflames it further.

Fulfilment of desire frees one from the tension that dopamine was creating in the brain. Plus, there is a momentary pleasure of the senses on coming in contact with their objects of desire. However, the pleasure does not last. It wanes like a passing comet.

Once the momentary feeling of enjoyment is gone, the mind again creates the desire so that it may experience that happiness again. This time, the desire is more intense than before because attachment has increased. Each time the desire returns, it is stronger than earlier, and in this way, craving sets in.

This is true no matter what object we crave. The brain registers all pleasure the same way, whether it originates from a delicious meal, a sexual encounter, a drug or a financial reward. Whenever we repeatedly strive to quench a desire, it grows into a craving. And if the craving is for a pleasure that is viewed by society as immoral, it gets labelled as an 'addiction'.

How Addiction Develops

The state of craving becomes an 'addiction' when it increases to the point that one loses control over the self. Addictions grip people so strongly that they ignore even extreme harm to indulge in them.

The etymology of the word 'addiction' in Latin implies 'enslaved by'.[4] If you have ever tried to help people with an addiction, or suffered from one yourself, you will understand why 'enslaved by' is so apt.

The influence of addiction manifests in the following three ways:

1. intense craving for the object of addiction;

2. loss of control in the ability to limit the number of times the object is used; and

3. continued craving for it despite facing adverse circumstances.

Initially, addiction gets triggered by repeated exposure to a pleasurable object and indulgence in it. But later, it gains hold as an altered state of the brain. Just as cardiovascular disease injures the heart, addiction modifies the functioning of the brain.

---

[4] Richard J Rosenthal and Suzanne B Faris, 'The Etymology and Early History of "Addiction"', Taylor & Francis Online, 5 Feb 2019, https://www.tandfonline.com/doi/full/10.1080/16066359.2018.1543412

Earlier, psychologists viewed addiction as ethically flawed behaviour arising from a psychological defect. Now consensus amongst the scientific community has changed. Addiction is seen as a chronic disease that goes beyond psychology, to physiology.[5]

Previously, the expert opinion was that only drugs and alcohol could cause addiction. Now, neuroimaging technologies have shown that any pleasurable activity can hijack the brain. This includes activities such as video gaming, gambling, shopping and even eating junk food.

The Physiology of Addiction

Dopamine's influence does not stop at creating the hope of pleasure; it trains the brain in reward-related learning. This reward system in our brain links activities with pleasure. It is necessary for survival because it links activities like eating and defending with reward. Thereby, it motivates us to engage in these works of daily maintenance.

But now, dopamine hijacks the brain and links pleasure to memories of fulfilment of desire. The brain keeps learning, to our detriment, that satiating our

---

[5] Eric D Morse, 'Addiction is a Chronic Medical Illness', National Library of Medicine, May-June 2018, https://pubmed.ncbi.nlm.nih.gov/29735618/

desire will result in pleasure. Consequently, the desire keeps getting deepened.

In life, rewards only come after persistent effort over time but addictive substances provide a shortcut. They flood the brain with dopamine and can release up to ten times the amount of dopamine that natural rewards do. Sadly, the brain has no easy way to withstand their onslaught, and the result is addiction to that pleasure.

The brain responds to this situation by producing less dopamine. It is similar to lowering the volume of a speaker when the noise is too high. Consequently, the amount of pleasure we get from the object now reduces. Earlier, a snort of heroin was adequate to feel the kick, but even an injection does not suffice now. Consequently, to experience the same amount of 'high', addicted people increase their consumption of the chemical.

At this stage, compulsion sets in. The pleasure continues to reduce, but the memory of the moment of gratification persists. The brain accesses memories of the situation in which the pleasure was savoured. These memories of the circumstances serve as sweet triggers. Whenever they are present, they activate the conditioned response of intense craving.

This also explains why people recently freed from addictions face danger in the face of the old triggers.

One who was previously addicted to alcohol will experience a pang of craving on seeing the bottle and is in danger of slipping back into the habit again. One who was enslaved by heroin faces the danger of relapsing into it, on seeing a hypodermic needle.

Shun Bad Association

It is said that the best time to get rid of an addiction is before it begins. Hence, Vedic scriptures caution us about the ill-effects of environments that expose us to addictive pleasures. We are advised to shun *kusang*, which is the opposite of satsang. What is *kusang*?

Just as satsang is good association that takes our mind to the divine, *kusang* is bad association that exposes us to addictive pleasures. It includes socialization with people engaging in substance abuse, gambling, intoxication and similar vices. The big danger in *kusang* is that it induces contemplation of happiness in harmful places. Then, before we realize it, the next step is cravings and addictions.

Teenagers are especially vulnerable to *kusang* because their pre-frontal cortex is not yet fully developed. When subject to peer pressure, they possess insufficient willpower to resist it. Hence, avoidance of such environment is the best policy.

The *Narad Bhakti Darshan* states:

duḥsaṅgaḥ sarvathaiva tyājyaḥ
kāmakrodhamohasmṛitibhraṁśha
*   buddhināśha sarvanāśhakāraṇatvāt*

(sutras 43–44)

In these aphorisms, Sage Narad has used strong words to warn us about the harmful effects of *kusaṅg*. He says: 'Bad association should be shunned by all means. It is the cause of desire, anger, delusion, loss of memory, loss of intellect and utter ruin.'

Empower Yourself with Divine Wisdom

The faulty structures were formed because of false understanding and incorrect beliefs, usually passed down for generations. The reason for them was lack of proper knowledge. We created desires in the pursuit of happiness without realizing we were searching in the wrong place.

Like the fly that came to eat honey and got stuck in it, we too got stuck in ever-increasing craving. Now, we must become wise to futile desires and how they trap us.

Insects living under stones are creatures of darkness. They dig burrows in the soil and are perfectly comfortable living there.

As a little child, during my summer vacation, I would sometimes play with my friends in the empty fields around our neighbourhood. One of our frivolous pastimes was to overturn medium-size stones and observe the commotion of the microhabitat of beetles, bugs, scorpions and centipedes.

The moment we removed the stone and allowed light to shine on these creatures of darkness, they would run helter-skelter for shelter. As mischievous children, watching them run would give us a kick.

Just as the vermin dwelling below stones cannot stand the light, likewise, pernicious thought structures in our mind must be dispelled with the light of knowledge.

In the material world, we turn to Google or friends and family for proper information. In the spiritual realm, one should seek proper knowledge from a Spiritual Master. The Bhagavad Gita states:

tad viddhi praṇipātena paripraśhnena sevayā
upadekṣhyanti te jñānaṁ jñāninas tattva-darśhinaḥ

(verse 4.34)

'Learn the Truth by approaching a Spiritual Master. Inquire from him with reverence and render service unto him. Such an enlightened saint can impart knowledge unto you because he has seen the Truth.'

The true Guru will enlighten us on the nature of the workings of the mind and how these can be rectified.

The purpose of life, however, is not just to rid ourselves of negative thought structures but to develop positive and divine ones. Let us now apply ourselves to this wonderful and fulfilling task.

7

Enrich Yourself in Solitude

At this point, we have covered about half of our journey through this book. We have gained a good measure of understanding of the maladies of thought. From this chapter onwards, we will start the second half of the journey towards developing lofty and noble emotions. So, tighten your seat belts as we take off and continue gaining altitude chapter-by-chapter.

Most of us love the joy of travelling to new places, discovering new locales and observing the panorama of life there. But I have heard of a tribe of Native American Indians who lived only a hundred miles away from the Pacific Ocean. Yet, they were unaware of the existence of the ocean. The reason? There was a mountain range between their village and the Pacific. They had never bothered to scale it to discover what lay beyond. If only they had possessed the spirit of exploration and adventure, it would have put them in

touch with the largest body of water on the planet and
changed the expanse of their thought horizons forever.

There is yet another pilgrimage, more exciting than
journeying to the Pacific, the Himalayas or Mars. It
is the excursion within our own self, which unearths
secrets related to the mysteries of the mind, intellect,
ego and soul. It is the most profitable expedition
we can undertake, for it reveals treasures within, of
everlasting joy. What a pity that so few are inspired to
embark on the inner journey! Or if they do, to persist
until the goal is reached.

This journey into our inner recesses is greatly
facilitated by the practice of solitude.

Favourite Pastime of Thought Leaders

Read the biographies of legendary figures who made a
huge impact on the world, and you will find that virtually
all of them spent considerable amounts of time 'thinking'
and planning in solitude. This includes social and political
leaders whose views changed the direction of humankind.
And, of course, the great prophets who uplifted the
lives of billions with their philosophies and teachings.
Consider the example of Sage Ved Vyas, whose birthday
is celebrated as Guru Purnima around the world.

Sage Krishna Dwaipayana Vyas's contribution
to Indian philosophy is unparalleled in history. Prior

to him, the Vedas had been passed down by the oral tradition, from master to disciple. He put them down in writing for the first time and also divided them into four—Rig Veda, Yajur Veda, Sama Veda and Atharva Veda. This is how he got the name 'Ved Vyas', meaning the divider of the Vedas.

Further, Ved Vyas wrote the Mahabharat, in which was enshrined the Bhagavad Gita. He wrote seventeen Puranas, such as the Padma Puran, Shiv Puran, Garud Puran, and so on. He then wrote the Brahma Sutras, which are also called 'Vedant', meaning the conclusion of the Vedas.

But even after writing so many scriptures, Ved Vyas was still dissatisfied. He sat down on the banks of the river Saraswati to contemplate the reason for his discontent. At that time, Sage Narad arrived and suggested he write a text that would describe selfless divine love for God.

To fulfil those instructions, Ved Vyas went into intense solitude. The Bhagavatam states:

apaśhyat puruṣhaṁ pūrvaṁ
    māyāṁ cha tad-apāśhrayām   (1.7.4)

In solitude, Ved Vyas first had darshan of God. He then had darshan of the Lord's material energy, maya. He saw souls suffering under the bondage of maya. That moved him to pity, and motivated by compassion, *he wrote the Shreemad Bhagavatam, the eighteenth Puran.*

Like Ved Vyas, **thousands of saints have lifted their thoughts to sublime heights in solitude. We too must invest some of our time in solitude if we wish to develop noble thoughts.** We do not have to go into the forest. Instead, for some time every day, we can go into the deep recesses of our own mind.

Benefits of Solitude

In today's world, technology is everywhere, and it is hardly surprising that our 'me time' has reduced. Digital devices make us feel connected to the world 24x7. Every time we get a chance to go running, we plug in our headphones. When we sit in the car, we listen to NPR or Radio Mirchi. Bluetooth speakers accompany us even to the shower.

The irony is that with all the noise and clamour blaring at us from virtual space, huge segments of the population feel lonelier than ever before. The reason for this loneliness is not lack of external company, but an internal disconnect. They make no time to sit down and connect with their own selves. Without it, they are unable to clarify their inner conflicts and nourish their soul.

Interestingly, when I suggest to people to spend time by themselves, many respond, 'I am too busy', 'I need to be productive' and so on. To them, I explain that adding a little solitude to their overfilled schedule is not a waste of time. In fact, the busier they are, the more they will benefit from quiet time.

Solitude Stimulates Our Parasympathetic System

We all have heard of the body's reaction to stress. The **fight-or-flight response** increases the adrenaline in the blood, causing the heartbeat and breathing rate to rise. Solitude does the reverse. It jumpstarts our parasympathetic nervous system, also called the rest-and-digest system.

You can think of the **rest-and-digest response** as an anti-adrenaline response. It happens when the brain perceives absolutely no need for fight or flight. It then signals the brain to conserve energy. Consequently, the muscles ease themselves, blood pressure decreases, and the heart slows down. The sphincter muscles in the gastrointestinal tract rest themselves. At the same time, intestinal and gland activity increases.

Solitude Allows Our Brain to Relax

The endless chatter of electronic media all around provides constant stimulation to the brain. However, an overworked brain that is always in the overactive mode gets worn down easily. As a sensitive organ, it needs rest to recuperate. Solitude helps us block out the street noise, traffic sounds, conversations, barking dogs and TV. This facilitates the brain's mending and relaxation. It allows the brain to unwind and reboot.

This is no different from the engines in our cars and the computers in our offices. Constant use, without interceding rest, leads to greater wear-and-tear. Just as they require regular shutting off, our body and mind, too, need the 'down time'.

Many people I know block their calendars for 'me time' either first thing in the morning or the last thing at night before going to bed. They switch off their mobile phones and are not accessible during these hours. They have learnt that some quality time spent in solitude makes them more productive throughout the day.

Solitude Promotes Syncing of Mind and Body

Life's demands force us into the hyper mode of aggressive attitudes and busy workdays. To meet the constant pressures on our time, we are always tilted forward. The mind runs at a hundred miles an hour, while the body hurries behind, to catch up.

In this situation, solitude allows us to get off the merry-go-round of daily life, so the body and mind can get back into sync.

Solitude Provides an Opportunity for Perspective

In the hassles of everyday problems, we spend much of our time in the crisis mode, putting out the daily blazes that arise. This constant firefighting makes our perspective myopic, while the big questions in life get pushed to the sidelines.

Coming to a standstill helps us step back from the hustle and bustle. We can then muse about the bigger picture: How does this work fit into my life goals? Are my actions in line with my deepest values? What is the purpose of life anyway? What are my most important duties? And so on.

Such contemplation facilitates developing a bird's eye view of matters.

Solitude Allows Us to Plan Our Life

We spend a lot of time planning parties and vacations. But how much time do we spend planning how to get the most out of life?

Quiet space provides us an opportunity to introspect and evaluate where we are in our journey versus where we wish to be. We can think about our priorities. Then, if necessary, we can reinvent ourselves and shift our priorities, before moving ahead.

Often, I hear the complaint: 'Productivity will suffer if I take time off from work.' In fact, the reverse is true.

Being constantly surrounded by people can actually kill productivity. By investing a little time in ourselves, we can perform much better. Pablo Picasso, the great painter, went to the extent of saying, 'Without great solitude no serious work is possible.'[1]

Nikola Tesla, a famous inventor, concurred: 'Originality thrives in seclusion, free of outside influences . . . Be alone, that is the secret of invention; be alone, that is when ideas are born.'[2]

Great writers, composers and artists all spent innumerable hours in self-isolation, exploring new ideas and possibilities. In the field of education as well, universities give their faculty time off so that apart from teaching, they may also think, research and write.

Set Up a Time for Solitude

When we talk of solitude, for many people, it conjures images of going on a solo trek for a fortnight or shutting oneself off in a cabin for a month or moving into a monastery. These activities can undoubtedly offer a sizeable dose of solitude, but such radical isolation is

---

[1] 'Nothing Can Be Accomplished Without Solitude', Quote Investigator, 16 December 2015, https://quoteinvestigator.com/2015/12/16/solitude/

[2] 'Nikola Tesla Quote # 50', Tesla Universe, accessed 25 August 2020, https://teslauniverse.com/nikola-tesla/quotes/50

not feasible for most of us, at least not on a regular basis.

Instead, we can integrate 'isolation hour' into our daily schedule itself. It does not require extra money or labour. Simply block a time during the day solely for the purpose of solitude. The Bhagavad Gita states:

vivikta-sevī laghv-āśhī
   yata-vāk-kāya-mānasaḥ
dhyāna-yoga-paro nityaṁ
   vairāgyaṁ samupāśhritaḥ (verse 18.52)

Lord Krishna explains that we ascend in life when we relish solitude, eat lightly, control body and mind, engage in meditation and practise dispassion.

The Bible too states: 'When thou prayest, enter into thy closet and lock thy door.' (Matthew 6:6)

Do note that this isolation hour is not necessarily without digital devices. In fact, many people find they get much more out of it while listening to bhajans. Likewise, other people find the best nourishment for their soul while singing kirtans in a group. Some find it easier to follow an online meditation. That is great! These activities, however, should be added only if they help our inner journey. They also qualify as solitude, provided they strengthen the sacred space of our mind. The goal should be to go within ourselves and align our thoughts with our highest purpose.

So, do enrich your life by savouring the solace of quietude every day. Theoretically, we can allocate any time of the day for such contemplation. Realistically, however, the demands of life require us to handle one urgent task after another. In the process, our spiritual practice gets squeezed out because the intellect does not view it as urgent.

To ensure that it is not sacrificed, we should set apart a fixed time slot for solitude on a daily basis. This becomes doubly advantageous because a habit kicks in. The moment the time of the day comes, the brain itself triggers the inspiration, 'It is time for sadhana (spiritual practice in solitude).'

Find a Place for Contemplation

We can also set up a special place for solitude. Do note that on visiting a temple, our mind naturally experiences peace. Our thoughts turn more sacred and reverential. When we go to the market, our thoughts turn to needs and requirements. And on a trip to the countryside, our thoughts slow down, while the mind takes on an expansive nature.

We can similarly create a sacred environment in our home by setting up a pooja room with an altar. After a few months, the environment will work as a trigger. Merely entering it will set off contemplative thoughts.

Blaise Pascal, the famous scientist and philosopher, had said, 'All of man's miseries derive from not being able to sit quietly in a room alone.'[3]

However, it is not necessary to shut yourself out physically. Some people find the most excellent isolation is when they take a walk by themselves. Mahatma Gandhi was famous for taking long walks. Albert Einstein said: 'I take time to go for long walks on the beach so that I can listen to what is going on inside my head.'[4] A.P.J. Abdul Kalam, the late Indian president, also loved walking for an hour every day.

You too can discover what activity works best to provide you the solitude you need. Let us now discuss some of the ways of utilizing our solitude.

Cultivate Introspection

Before we strive for self-development, we must take stock of the present nature of our thoughts. This is done through introspection. It means turning our attention to our inner states, to observe our thoughts and feelings. This puts us in touch with our shortcomings

[3] Robin Sharma, 'Learn to Meditate', New Indian Express, 11 October 2014, https://www.newindianexpress.com/cities/bengaluru/2014/oct/11/Learn-to-Meditate-670253.html

[4] Akash Majumdar, 'The Secret to Finding the Best Out of You', Medium, 15 Nov 2019, https://medium.com/@akashmajumder0303/what-brings-the-best-out-of-you-36146bc05b31

and deficiencies. Only then can we get into a position of setting realistic goals for the future.

Atma nirīkṣhaṅ (self-introspection) is also important because it enables us to better understand ourselves, with our unique traits and weaknesses. We become more aware of what we are good at, while acknowledging what we still need to learn. We then take responsibility for our mistakes and admit when we do not have the answers.

This seems counter-intuitive in the modern corporate environment, where everyone puts on an air of knowing everything. People fear others will judge them and question their abilities. That kind of pretence may be acceptable in the professional world, but not for self-improvement.

In introspection, we do a self-evaluation of the defects we need to overcome and areas we must grow in. We also become aware of our goal in life, and the distance we need to traverse to reach it. Then, with great inspiration, we move ahead on the inner journey.

8

Practise to Achieve Mastery

People are born with different innate talents and propensities. But no matter how great one's latent talents may be, the only way to manifest them as abilities is through practise.

Major Dhyan Chand is widely regarded as the greatest player in the history of field hockey.[1] As a member of the Indian team, he won three successive gold medals in the 1928, 1932 and 1936 Olympics. His hockey skills were so remarkable that his fans called him 'The Magician' and 'The Wizard'.

He was famous for his extraordinary goal-scoring abilities. In the 1928 Olympics, he was the highest scorer in the tournament with 14 goals. At the 1932 Olympics in Los Angeles, India defeated hosts US in

---

[1] 'Biography Dhyan Chand', Olympics, https://olympics.com/en/athletes/dhyan-chand-singh

the finals with a score of 24–1, of which 8 goals were netted by Chand.

Subsequently, he led the Indian team to the Berlin Olympics in 1936. This time, India played hosts Germany in the finals, and defeated them 8–1. Dhyan Chand's contribution was 3 goals. Hitler was watching the match along with 40,000 Germans. He was so impressed by the hockey stalwart's wizardry that he offered him German citizenship and the position of a colonel in his army, which Dhyan Chand politely refused, with the words, 'India is not for sale'.

What was the secret behind Dhyan Chand's superhuman skills in hockey? No doubt, he had natural talent. But beyond that, it was his intense determination to train himself. He would place the ball on the railway track and run with it for a mile. Daytime practise did not suffice for him; he wanted to continue at night as well. When the moon became visible at nightfall, he would go to the field and continue his training under the moonlight.

Enrolled in the Indian army, he lived in the barracks. His original name was Dhyan Singh. But seeing his obsession for practising under the moon, his fellow army men used to call him 'Chand', which means moon. That is how he came to be known as Dhyan Chand.

The takeaway from his amazing life story is his dedication to training. It would not be an exaggeration to say that nobody ever became an expert without adequate training.

Practise is the Key

You must have seen jugglers. They amaze people with their coordinated hand movements, making objects fly up to the exact height in the exact trajectory. They possess immaculate precision in throwing and catching, for even a slight mistake will mess it all up. But how do they perfect their act to such a level of accuracy? It is the result of practise, more practise, and even more practise.

Bruce Lee, one of the greatest martial arts virtuosos of all time, said: 'I fear not the man who has practised ten thousand kicks once. I fear the man who has practised one kick ten thousand times.'[2]

Physical expertise of the kind described above comes by training the brain. And the same feature can be tapped to train mental abilities. Let me share my own story of how practise helped in my journey as a public speaker.

---

[2] Jaana Bohr, '5 Business Lessons I've Learned From Martial Arts', LinkedIn, 16 April 2019, https://www.linkedin.com/pulse/5-business-lessons-ive-learned-from-martial-arts-jaana-hein/

You might have visited our channel on YouTube and enjoyed the videos posted there by the JKYog media team. But let me tell you that public-speaking skills did not just fall into my lap. In fact, you may not believe me when I tell you this, but the first time I tried speaking in public, I was embarrassingly awful.

It was about three and a half decades ago. I was residing at the ashram with my Spiritual Master, learning the Vedic scriptures under his expert and loving tutelage. His instruction to me was that apart from daily meditation and contemplation, I must study the scriptures and internalize the knowledge for twelve hours a day. That left me with little time for anything else.

However, I soon realized that to disseminate the knowledge I was cultivating, I would also need to learn public speaking. When I tried it—I would speak to the wall since there was no public there—I realized how absolutely pathetic I was at it. The content was in my head, but the delivery was skewed; the voice modulations were not just unimpressive but monotonous; they could put anyone to sleep.

Now what to do? There were only two options. Either lose heart and give up, or practise really hard in the hope that improvement would happen. So, I procured recordings (in cassette tapes) of speeches made by good speakers. I needed to hear how they spoke and learn from them.

Since there was no free time in my schedule to hear the tapes, I would carry my meal from the dining room to my room. There, I would listen to the tapes while eating. Now, with food in my mouth, it was not possible to practise verbally. So, while listening to a speech, I would mentally speak alongside. I followed this system diligently for months.

For the first few weeks, nothing happened. I remained as terrible at lecturing as ever. But then, slowly, the needle started shifting. Months went by and the change was substantial. And finally, after a year, when I completed my studies, I was happy that I had reached a level of proficiency where nobody could say, 'He is a bad speaker'.

Only much later did I come to know that the process I had adopted was known technically as 'deliberate practise'. What is this process and how is it different from ordinary practise?

'Deliberate' Practise versus Mindless Repetition

Millions of golfers practise their game every week. But after fifty years of play, their golf does not improve. Why does the practise not benefit them despite the thousands of hours spent playing? The reason is that it is mindless repetition, without enough attention on improvement.

Deliberate practise, in contrast, is highly focused. In it, we execute each repetition with the express intention of improving. We aim at ironing out our weaknesses. And we exert our abilities to learn and progress beyond previous levels. This forces our brain to engage more of its areas and rewire itself to enhance our skill set. That is why deliberate practise is so exhausting that athletes often go to sleep at the end of such sessions. They feel tired, not just physically, but emotionally and intellectually as well. And yet, this is exactly the kind of drill that brings about massive improvement.

Virat Kohli, former captain of India's cricket team, explained his strategy for deliberate practise. Every time he goes for net practise, he does not just enjoy hitting the ball. Rather, he is completely focused on improving a specific aspect of his game by the end of the two-hour session.[3]

As with physical adroitness, for mental mastery too, we must commit ourselves to purposeful training. Let us first take a closer look at the learning process of the brain.

---

[3] Shreyas Sharma, 'Virat Kohli Keen on Improving His Game', India Today, 15 June 2012, https://www.indiatoday.in/sports/cricket/story/virat-kohli-keen-on-improving-his-game-105811-2012-06-15

How the Brain Learns

In learning any skill, we progress through three stages. The **first stage is conscious incompetence**. At this stage, we exert our conscious mind to perform an activity, and yet are inept at it. For example, when children first sit on a bicycle, they find it a complex task. They are required to maintain balance, push the pedals, grip the handle and look ahead. They exert their full intellect and yet fall.

With practise, we reach the **second stage, which is conscious competence**. We are now adept at the activity, but only when we fully engage our conscious mind in it. In the bicycle example, children can now ride it without falling, but they need to pay complete attention to it.

Further practise brings us to the **third stage, which is unconscious competence**. At that stage, the subconscious mind takes over, and we are able to perform the task without active engagement of the conscious mind. Thus, after a few weeks of cycling, children can now even talk to friends alongside. The point of automaticity is reached, where the activity is being performed on autopilot.

How does practise bring the state of automaticity? It strengthens the neural pathways of the brain. As the popular saying goes: 'neurons that fire together wire together'. Thus, the brain gets rewired to perform the task more easily.

Hebbian Theory of Neuroscience

Donald Hebb, a neurologist, was the first to postulate how neurons are rewired. His ideas are now widely accepted as the Hebbian theory of learning. This theory states that when an axon of neuron A repeatedly excites neuron B, and persistently fires it, an organic change happens in both. This enhances neuron A's efficiency in firing neuron B.[4]

Consequently, neurons that repeatedly fire at the same time tend to become 'associated'. Thereby, activity in one facilitates activity in the other. It results in the learning process, which enables us to master any skill. The same principle holds for any activity, such as typing, driving, music and so on.

The Hebbian theory can also explain why lack of revision leads to forgetfulness. If the neural networks created are not utilized for a long time, they revert to their previous state. Thus, without practise, proficiency

---

[4] Jesse J Langille and Richard E Brown, 'The Synaptic Theory of Memory: A Historical Survey and Reconciliation of Recent Opposition', National Library of Medicine, 26 Oct 2018, https://www.ncbi.nlm.nih.gov/pmc/articles/PMC6212519/

in any field gets rusted. The *Hitopadesh* warns us of the same:

anabhyāsena viṣaṁ vidyā, hyajīrṇe bhojanaṁ viṣham
viṣaṁ sabhā daridrasya, vṛiddhasya taruṇī viṣham

'Without revision, knowledge turns toxic. On eating without appetite, food turns into poison. The assembly of scholars is noxious to a fool. While a young damsel seems venomous to an old man.'

In case we forget previous learning due to negligence, there is still hope. When we again begin revision, the synaptic learning process is much quicker than the first time. Consequently, we can pick up the skill again very quickly. Then, by revising what we have learnt, the neural structures continue intact, and the knowledge stays fresh in our intellect.

Learning is Possible Even When Neurons Have Maxed Out

There is a paradox to learning. On the one hand, as per medical science, the brain develops to its maximum size by the age of twenty-five, after which there is very little increase in grey and white matter. And yet, people keep learning new skills and disciplines all their life.

Peter Drucker is considered by many as the founder of modern management[5]. His writings contributed to the philosophical and practical foundations of the modern business corporation. He invented the management technique known as MBO or Management by Objectives.

Drucker was the first to predict the emergence of the information society with its necessity for lifelong learning. He coined the term 'knowledge worker' that is popularly used today.

Drucker was a lifelong learner himself. Every three years, he would pick up a new subject, be it Japanese art, the theory of music, or rural economics. He felt it forced him to be open to new disciplines, methods and approaches. He continued this habit into his nineties, until his physical health did not permit it any longer. He taught his last class at ninety-two, three years before his death at ninety-five.

Drucker's case illustrates the potential we humans possess for learning new skills almost until death. When the quantity of brain matter has stopped growing, what provides the ability to learn ever-new things even in old age?

---

[5] 'Peter Drucker', Drucker Institute, https://www.drucker.institute/perspective/about-peter-drucker/

The answer is that although the number of neurons max out with age, their ability to wire up amongst themselves remains. They can thus form new circuits leading to new skills. As the saying goes: 'you are never too old to learn'.

Having understood the learning process, we will now see how these principles can be utilized in coaching our mind.

Train Your Thoughts

The neural learning nature of the brain applies to our thoughts as well. Every time we think, it creates a pattern of neural firings. When we repeat the same thought again and again, the neurons wire up to create a neural highway. The particular thought now comes as if automatically to us.

Thus, the emotions we frequently indulge in become our attitudes. For example, if we continually focus on inspiring thoughts, we develop an inspired mindset. If we regularly bring to our mind the trait of positivity, we develop a positive personality. Understand it through this story.

Sanjeev Khanna attended JKYog's Life Transformation Programme and got inspired. He thought, 'I have understood the importance of human life. I must now use the precious opportunity it presents to achieve the supreme destination for my soul. From tomorrow, I will begin my spiritual practice as it was described in the lecture.'

That night, at 10 p.m., Sanjeev set his alarm for 4 a.m. the next day. By waking up early, he would get two hours for sadhana.

The next morning, the alarm rang, 'Krinnng.' Sanjeev was jolted straight from the dream state to the waking state. 'Who is disturbing me?' he screamed, and shutting the alarm off, he went right back to sleep.

The next time Sanjeev's eyes opened, he was shocked to see that he had slept till 7.30 a.m. 'Oh no!' he exclaimed. 'This is terrible. I slept through the morning and missed my chance for sadhana. If I stay lazy like this, how will I ever transform myself?' In this way, he regretted his actions deeply, mentally revising thoughts of repentance with intensity.

That night at 10 p.m., he again set the alarm for 4 a.m. The next morning, as expected, again the alarm went off, 'Krinnng'.

'Argh! So frustrating!' Sanjeev screamed. He shut off the alarm and went right back to sleep.

However, he heard a heavy banging on the door at 4.05 a.m. He sat up in bed and realized that someone was pounding on the door. This time there was no way of shutting it off. 'Okay, okay . . . I am coming,' he shouted. 'Why are you banging on the door like this?'

Nevertheless, the banging continued. Sanjeev opened the door and discovered a wretched-looking man standing outside, wearing a black cape. The man had bloodshot eyes, white horns on his head, black paint smeared on his face and a trident in his hand.

'Who are you?' asked Sanjeev.

'I am Pāp Purush (sin personified),' replied the man.

'Pāp Purush! Yes, you look like that,' Sanjeev exclaimed. But then a question came to his mind and he blurted, 'If you are Pāp Purush, then why have you come to wake me up? Your interest will be served if I keep sleeping.'

'The problem is,' answered Pāp Purush, 'that yesterday when you did not wake up on time, you repented so deeply. You ruminated on purifying thoughts over and over again. As a result, all the members of my family, such as Procrastination and Pride, died within your heart. Now, I am worried that if you do not wake up today either, you will again start the same chintan. Then I too will have no place left in your heart. That is why I have come to rouse you.'

The story graphically illustrates the power of repetition of thoughts. Maharshi Patanjali emphasizes training the mind through practise:

tatra sthitau yatno 'bhyāsaḥ   (*Yog Darshan* sutra 1.13)

'*Abhyās* (practise) is the steadfast effort to control the mind.'

Chintan—the Most Powerful Tool in Our Armoury

In Sanskrit, mental practise is called *chintan*. It means 'deep reflective thought'. *Chintan* is one of the most potent life transformation tools available to humans. Its power arises from the repetition of a thought again and again. For lack of awareness of its potential, we do not sufficiently tap into it.

Every year when the school board exam results are declared, thousands of students fail them.

On learning that they failed, some students contemplate, 'This is a wake-up call for me. My parents are spending so much upon me; I do not wish to waste their money. Next year, I will work harder and pass the exam.'

But a few brooded, 'I have failed. How will I show my face to my friends? What will my parents say?' and so on. Consequently, the chintan *grips the mind so strongly, that it goes into a negative downward spiral. The student then concludes it is not possible for him to live and swallows poison.*

Imagine how powerful negative *chintan* is that it can bring people to the point of suicide. A popular Sanskrit verse states:

> *chintā chitā samākhyātā, chintā chitātodhikā*
> *chitā dahati nirjīvam, chintā jīvama hi dahyati*
>
> (*Sukti Sudhakar*)

'*Chintā* (worry) and the *chitā* (funeral pyre) both burn a person. The difference is that while fire burns the dead body, worry burns us while we are alive.' This is the impact of negative contemplation.

Conversely, positive contemplation can lift our mind to sublime heights. It can even make us meet God. All we need to do is to dwell on the thought: 'Lord Krishna is mine. He is the Abode of divine virtues. He is causelessly merciful. He is my eternal Father.' With sufficient repetitions, our mind will become bathed in divine love, and we will attract His divine grace.

The mind takes on the nature of whatever it contemplates. Philosophers and writers concur with this principle. Ralph Waldo Emerson said: 'You become what you think all day long.'[6] And Earl Nightingale said: 'You do become what you think about.'[7]

Hence, **the nature of our *chintan* determines what we become in life.** This knowledge provides us with an easy tool for transforming our life: **Improve your *chintan* to improve your life.**

Here are some strategies for training your thoughts.

Think Intentionally

So far, we let thoughts happen to us. Situations cause thoughts to arise as an automated response. In intentional thinking, we disregard the programmed response and instead, consciously choose our thoughts.

First, we ask ourselves, 'How would I like to feel in this situation?' Possibly, more relaxed, more focused, or more loving? Great! Now the goal is set. We have defined the emotions we would like to have.

Next, we exert control over the mind and brain to create those sentiments. This is intentional thinking, where we put in a conscious effort to think beautiful,

---

[6] Liza Ferentz, 'You Are What You Think', Psychology Today, 20 March 2017, https://www.psychologytoday.com/us/blog/healing-trauma-s-wounds/201703/you-are-what-you-think

[7] Peter Economy, '37 Earl Nightingale Quotes That Will Empower You to Soar High', Inc., 2 Oct 2015, https://www.inc.com/peter-economy/37-earl-nightingale-quotes-that-will-empower-you-to-soar-high.html

positive and beneficial thoughts. Such emotions that will help us grow.

This may seem unfamiliar, if you have not engaged in intentional thinking before. Doing it can give rise to an all-new feeling, much like exploring the scenery from a new mountain range for the first time. But as you persevere, it will begin to feel natural.

Then, start putting more energy into your intentionality. Focus on the deliberate thoughts you bring to your mind and put more life into them. Add feelings and emotions.

Revise the Desirable Thoughts

This is the tough part. Just as any kind of practise is difficult, mental practise is also a laborious task. It requires forcing the uncooperative mind. That is why people either become lazy or lose heart.

Nonetheless, like any other learning process, we must push ourselves past the complaining mind. The more we practise this kind of contemplative thinking, the better we will become at it. The mind becomes nimbler and more disciplined; it begins to cooperate with our commands. So, let us try to exercise this faculty every day.

The emotion or thought we revise depends upon what we wish to achieve. It could be used as a tool to overcome defects. For example:

- *I must not be judgmental. I do not know people's story.*

- *Being resentful will only hurt me. I must see pain as an opportunity for growth. As the adage goes: 'no pain, no gain'.*

- *Jealousy blocks the grace of God. I should rejoice when I see the success of others because God resides in them too.*

Similarly, *chintan* could be used as a tool for developing virtues:

- *I will be brave and courageous because God's grace is with me.*

- *I must develop inner strength and learn to persevere. I will not give up in the face of challenges.*

- *Humility attracts divine grace. Just as the firefly in front of the sun, I too am insignificant in front of God.*

Once you have tapped into the power of *chintan*, you will appreciate that **when it comes to self-development, the sky is the limit. If we have sufficient desire and are willing to put in the necessary mental practise, we can lift our mind to unimaginable heights.** But for that to happen, we must commit to the self-discipline required for rigorous mental training.

Even with a little practise, we will taste the enormous power of thoughts. Until now, thinking was happening to us. But now, we make thoughts happen. And this brings us to the next stage.

Think New Thoughts

If you are like most people, you love to try out new things—new places to eat, new clothes to wear and new movies to see. How about extending the practice to thoughts as well? Try newer ways of thinking. For example:

Instead of 'I can never lose weight'.
Think 'If I work at it, I can surely become slim and trim'.

Instead of 'Work is so boring'.
Think 'Work is so enjoyable and fulfilling'.

Instead of 'My spouse does not take care of me'.
Think 'My spouse is there so that I can love him'.

Instead of 'I do not know what will happen in future'.
Think 'The future will be much better than the past'.

Instead of 'If people do not like me, I will be devastated'.
Think 'The worst that can happen is a feeling'.

Instead of 'Improvement requires too much hard work'.
Think 'The pain of growth is much better than the pain of stagnation'.

Notice how your feelings change as you change your thoughts. With practise, you will discover that not only do you experience positive thoughts more often, but they also start becoming more insightful.

Feed Your Mind

Common sense informs us that our body is made from what we eat. We cannot continuously eat unhealthy food, which is high in sugar and fat, and yet hope to remain healthy. Wise people, therefore, desist from consuming 'junk food'.

The same principle applies to the mind too. The difference is that we feed our body through the mouth, but we feed our mind through all our five senses. Gossip, crime stories, explicit pictures, etc., are all 'junk food' for the mind. Deplorably, headlines of print media highlight the worst in humankind. The news programmes constantly rant about how bad things are and how much worse they are heading to be.

If we are not careful, the worthless banter on social media and political debates on TV will become fodder for our head. Then, do not be surprised if the garbage in your head feeds you with pessimism and dismay. Instead, if we wish to develop a mind that can take us on sublime flights of thought, we must carefully watch the diet we provide it.

That is why Mahatma Gandhi popularized the idea of the three monkeys: 'hear no evil; see no evil; speak no evil'. Take a pause here and ponder over what you allowed into your mind today.

Good *sādhaks* (spiritual aspirants) carefully guard the gateway of their mind. Even better is to proactively feed the mind a good diet of wisdom, inspiration and knowledge. You can get this by reading good books and listening to educational videos. Modern technology provides the opportunity to listen to lectures on your morning drive and evening walks. People who get great ideas and innovative inspirations are the ones who nourish their mind daily with divine wisdom.

Physical Exercise

It may not be obvious, but spirited exercise for half an hour releases endorphins in the brain, which are pleasure chemicals. These can supercharge our thinking. It also releases Brain-Derived Neurotrophic Factor (BDNF), which helps the brain's health. Read the daily routine of Viswanathan Anand, the former world chess champion, and you will understand the emphasis he laid on regular exercise.

A great exercise is brisk walking. It enables the mind to calm down and get the most out of your thinking. Playing an organized sport is okay but exercising by yourself is even better. It gives your mind the solitude to get the most out of your thought process. Many luminaries renowned for their creative thinking had the habit of taking long walks.

In the yoga and meditation workshops I conduct, I teach **Kripalu-Prakriya: Three Steps to Holistic Health**. It is a one-hour system of physical practice.

20 minutes: yogasanas (including stretches, flexes and muscle exercises)

10 minutes: pranayam (*Bhastrikā, Nādī Shodhan, Kapal Bhātī, Bhrāmarī*)

30 minutes: walking/running/cardio

----

60 minutes—Total duration

Spiritual Exercise

Just as we invest time in keeping our body healthy, we must also invest time in keeping our mind healthy. This is accomplished through spiritual exercise.

I teach an easy system for integrating sadhana into your daily life, with the **Kripalu-Padhati: Three Steps to Mind Management**. It is a one-hour format for devotional practice.

5 minutes: daily prayer

10 minutes: Roop Dhyan meditation

20 minutes: listen to a lecture

20 minutes: kirtan (chanting meditation)

5 minutes: *Āratī* (ceremony of lights)

----

60 minutes—Total duration

We have now begun tapping into the positive power of thoughts. In the next chapter, we will learn to hone the concentration of our thoughts on the subject of our choice.

9

Focus Your Thoughts

The human mind is an amazing piece of equipment. Like a supercomputer, it is capable of analysing the most complex problems. It accesses tomes of information to create a single thought or feeling. Yet, to prevent squandering away its potential, we must train it well in the art of thinking. And an important part of training the mind is developing focus.

What is focus? It can be defined as keeping the beam of our attention on the subject of our choice for extended periods of time. Focusing our mind on an activity multiplies the energy we bear upon it. In this chapter, we will learn the value of focus and ways to improve it.

The Importance of Focus

Consider the example of the sun. It is a huge reservoir of power. It radiates billions of kilowatts of energy upon the earth every minute. Yet, you can take a light umbrella and walk under the sun for hours without suffering from burns.

In contrast, a laser beam is a tiny source of energy. It merely directs a few watts of power into a focused beam of light. And yet, it is effectively used for laparoscopic surgery in humans. In fact, laser beams are even employed in drilling holes in diamonds.

The difference between sunlight and a laser beam is in the extent of focus. With concentration, we can create intensity in any physical or mental activity we perform. Hence, if we wish to hone our musical technique, we must focus our mind on it with deep attention. Similarly, to perform well at a job interview, you must focus and think to the best of your ability.

Focus Removes Mental Clutter

Have you ever driven through a snowstorm? Let me share my personal experience.

A few years ago, I was in Albany, in upstate New York, for a week-long programme. It was early April, and an out-of-season snowstorm hit us. Consequently, at night when we walked out of the building to the porch, the blizzard was in full fury.

To further complicate matters, my host was an eighty-year-old gentleman. With his glasses, night-time driving in that storm would be a nightmare so I offered to drive. For the next hour, with the snowflakes blowing on to the windscreen, visibility was only fifteen per cent. We kept crawling forward at twenty miles an hour. Finally, when we reached his garage, I was relieved after the craziest drive of my life.

Similarly, if we seek deep comprehension of a subject, we must put aside our mental clutter and then pay complete attention to it. We must not absentmindedly engage our subconscious, but the full force of our conscious mind. This is focused thinking.

Focus Facilitates Understanding

Suppose we are listening to a talk and wish to understand it deeply, we cannot allow our mind to wander. Rather, we must focus our complete attention upon what is being said. Then, our mind will shift from being extensive to being selective.

Sharp focus will bring all our mental energies to bear on the subject at hand. Focused thinking was what we used when we studied literally any subject, all the way from primary school to graduation.

Focus Improves Our Emotional State

Greater focus means greater control over the thoughts in our mind. While earlier, thinking happened to us, now we choose how we wish to feel. Thus, by choosing better emotions, our psychological state improves. We develop confidence in our abilities and optimism at work.

The positive state then translates to increased effectivity in everything we do. We feel in charge of our life. This in turn empowers us to plan our time better and be more productive.

Focus Helps Upgrade Our Skill Set

We can never perfect any skill if we practise it with diluted attention. The reason is that our mind and intellect can only pay full attention to one subject at a time. But if we have developed our focus, we can kick off all competing thoughts, thereby enabling the mind to perform at its best. If, however, our focus is distracted, we lose control and our performance deteriorates.

Focus Helps Us Attain God

Ultimately, the goal of life is to attain the Supreme Lord. That can only happen when our mind attains complete and absolute absorption in the Divine. The Bhagavad Gita explains:

> 'Just as a lamp in a windless place does not flicker, so the disciplined mind of a yogi remains steady in meditation on the Supreme. When the mind, restrained from material activities, becomes still by the practice of Yog, then the yogi is able to behold the soul through

the purified mind, and he rejoices in the inner joy. In that joyous state of Yog, called samadhi, one experiences supreme boundless divine bliss, and thus situated, one never deviates from the Eternal Truth.' (verses 6.19–21)

Hence, the aim of spiritual practice is to develop the ability of the mind to focus on the divine realm by various ways, such as ashtang yog, bhakti yog, hatha yog or jnana yog.

The Problem of Distraction

Every morning, on waking up, we get 86,400 seconds to live. One by one, the moments go by and nothing on earth can bring them back. The wealthy cannot buy more of these moments, while the poor do not get less. The only choice we have is how to spend them. In this scenario, if we wish to create the life we want, we will have to become extremely good at saying 'No' to a thousand distractions.

Unfortunately, many of us have great difficulty denying the demands on our time. And this dilutes our focus. Sometimes we are scared of straining a relationship. Other times we say 'Yes' even to strangers, just to keep up appearances. On yet other occasions, we succumb to peer pressure.

Another factor that breaks our focus is our propensity for distractions, whether it is through social media, the Internet or TV. Ubiquitous access to the Internet and faster data speeds mean that distractions are more accessible today than ever before. Technology has both empowered us and dispersed our focus all over the place.

In earlier eras, one had to search for diversions with much effort. But in the twenty-first century, they are just a click of the mouse away, and it is easy to fall prey to them. When we allow our mind the repeated luxury of distractions, it becomes conditioned to seeking constant stimulation. Every time the work at hand seems a bit boring, our brain seeks a dopamine hit by surfing the news or catching up on WhatsApp.

Research studies reveal that people working on computers keep multiple screens open simultaneously. Added to it is the distraction from the smartphone that is always at hand. In a day's work, people switch windows 566 times. That amounts to rotating their attention 566 times amongst different tasks. On average, they remain on one task for only forty-five seconds, before diverting their attention to an email, WhatsApp message, social media and the like. People may claim they are multitasking, but the quality of work suffers in the process because our attention span has its limitations.[1]

Our Attention Span

The environment constantly bombards us with information in the form of sounds, sights, messages, etc. Professor Timothy Wilson of the University of Virginia estimated that we receive eleven million bits of information in the form of sensory experience every second.[2]

But at any given time, our brain can consciously process only a few pieces of information. Again, Prof. Wilson estimated that forty bits of information at a time is the average limit of our mind's attention span. Consequently, there is often an information overload leading to absent-mindedness.

The Problem of Absent-mindedness

Have you ever walked to your bedroom to get something but on reaching there, you forgot why you

---

[1] Leo Yeykelis, James J. Cummings, Byron Reeves, 'Multitasking on a Single Device: Arousal and the Frequency, Anticipation, and Prediction of Switching Between Media Content on a Computer', Journal of Communication, 7 January 2014, https://academic.oup.com/joc/article-abstract/64/1/167/4085996

[2] Jane Porter, 'You're More Biased Than You Think', Fast Company, 6 Oct 2014, https://www.fastcompany.com/3036627/youre-more-biased-than-you-think

had come? The reason was that while walking, you were also speaking on your mobile and thinking about office work. These other things filled your attention span.

Texting while driving is prohibited for the same reason—it crams our attentional space. If our focus is diverted to the mobile, attention on driving suffers, leading to a greater risk of accidents.

Similarly, while reading a book, we focus our attention on its sentences. But sometimes, the mind wanders and begins to think of other things. Then, what we read gets blanked out. We have to return to the same sentences again, this time with greater focus. The problem of distraction happens because only a fraction of our mind is on the subject, while a major portion is elsewhere.

Habitual versus Attentional Tasks

We perform some tasks as a matter of habit like gardening, washing clothes, making coffee and so on. These do not require the complete attention of our conscious mind. We have performed them so often in the past that they are now automated. Even if the conscious mind gets diverted, the subconscious mind can continue the task. This is why, while driving, we can still engage in an animated conversation with fellow passengers.

Conversely, many activities cannot be performed by habit like listening to a discourse, giving a talk, or preparing a project report. These tasks require the full attention of our conscious mind. They are impeded by distractions that are all around us. If we can develop the ability for intense concentration, we will become more effective individuals. What is the way to do it?

To enhance our concentration, we must avoid two kinds of distractions. First are external distractions coming from the mobile, TV, etc. Second are the distracting thoughts from within.

Dealing with External Distractions

The novelty bias of our brain is what makes us vulnerable to distractions. When work and chores become boring, a change in tasks rewards the brain with a dopamine kick. This provides gratification to the mind and an escape from the boredom of work. Thus, once the distraction is before us, it becomes a challenge to avoid it. The best time to protect ourselves from it is in advance. That means putting the object of distraction away.

Difficult times call for strong remedies. We must not hesitate to adopt harsh strategies for protecting our mental peace. The digital gadgets we possess are meant for our assistance, not the other way around. Unfortunately, instead of utilizing technology, we have become slaves to it. Many people wake up in the morning and before anything else, they look at the latest updates on their mobile. This can be effectively amended by creating self-imposed rules.

For example, one could resolve not to use the mobile between 8 p.m. and 8 a.m., thereby freeing up the morning and night hours for introspective work. Similarly, one could cancel the subscription to apps like Netflix, Jio, etc. and limit the number of times one checks emails and messages while working. Nowadays, there are anti-distraction apps that can be set to effectively block messages when focused work is to be done.

Dealing with Internal Distractions

For our scattered state of mind, we love to blame our smartphones, Bollywood and video games. These are no doubt the instruments of distraction. The biggest culprit, however, is within us. What is that?

It is the pleasure-seeking nature of our mind that pursues gratification and shirks from pain. If we can stamp it out with determination, it will enhance our control over the mind. We will then find a tremendous surge in our ability to resist all kinds of allurements.

Think of Your Mind as a Muscle

The process of muscle strengthening is easy to understand. The bodily muscles have limited strength and stamina. If unused, they begin to atrophy. But when exerted with vigorous and purposeful exercise, they get strengthened. In a physical workout, therefore, the goal is to exert yourself to the utmost. The more you can go beyond the discomfort, the more the muscles have to work themselves.

To tone your physique, you may have worked out with weights or seen others do it. The principle behind weight training is that muscles are built by challenging and exerting them. It then takes forty-eight hours for them to recover. With proper nutrition, they regenerate and grow stronger than before.

Developing the power of concentration works in the same fashion. The mind complains when we exert it and challenge it. But we must go beyond the boredom and the pain. Then, slowly the muscle of focus starts growing. The *Yog Sutras* state:

shraddhā vīrya smriti samādhi
prajñāpūrvaka itareṣām   (sutra 1.20)

'Practice must be pursued with faith, valour, keen memory, absorption and intelligence.'

Just as one never builds muscles by lounging on a couch all day, we will never develop the power of concentration by whiling away our time in light entertainment. Just as physical exercise demands hard work, mental exercise also requires hard work.

Your Attention Muscle Will Grow Gradually

If you wish to run long distance, you do not directly enter the marathon. You begin with running a mile on the first day and incrementally increase it over months and years. Likewise, if the attention muscle is flabby, do not expect it to suddenly run the mind marathon!

In the beginning of your practice, be prepared for the mind to get distracted from time to time. But the important thing is to keep at it. Maharshi Patanjali states:

sa tu dīrgha-kāla nairantarya-
 satkārāsevito dṛiḍhabhūmiḥ   (sutra 1.14)

'When practice is continued for a long duration with dedication, and without interruption, it becomes firmly grounded.'

With repeated exertion, the muscle of your mind will start budging. And one day, you will be amazed at how easy it has become. The focused mind will then be at your command, and you will find you can play better, work better and engage in your devotion better.

Concentration can be practised while performing any work that requires mental focus. But if you would like to practise through a suitable meditation, here is a sample exercise for growing your concentration.

Meditation with Every Breath

The great saints of India have given us an easy way of chanting the Name of the Lord. They teach us to recite His divine Names, as we inhale and exhale, with every breath. That is what we will meditate upon. You are welcome to choose any name of God that you wish, such as 'Radhey Krishna', 'Sita Ram' or 'Namah Shivaya'.

The Supreme Divine Personality is all-pure, and when we absorb our mind in Him, it gets purified as well. But how do we absorb our mind in Him? The *Padma Puran* declares that God is fully present in His Name. Hence, we can easily meditate upon Him by remembering His Name.

Let us now remember the divine Names of God with every breath.

Meditation Steps:

1. Sit cross-legged or in any comfortable posture. If sitting on the floor is uncomfortable for you, seat yourself on a chair.

2. Keep your back and neck straight.

3. Close your eyes for the duration of the meditation.

4. Relax your body and calm your mind.

5. Begin breathing deeply. Observe the breath as it flows in from the nostrils into the lungs, and from the lungs out through the nostrils.

6. Now imagine there are two pipes from your nostrils all the way to your stomach. Keep breathing steadily and visualize the breath moving through the pipes.

7. Add another element to the meditation. As you inhale, think that the name 'Radhey' flows in from the nostrils and travels down to the stomach. As you exhale, recall the name 'Krishna' flowing up from your stomach and out of the nostrils.

8. Continue meditating on the flowing breath, and along with it, on the Name of God. Add another thought to it: 'The divine Names are imbued with all the energies of the Lord. They are purifying my body and mind.'

9. Then, discard the pipes from your mind and just concentrate on the Name of God, 'Radhey Krishna, Radhey Krishna, Radhey Krishna . . .' Feel the Name traversing within yourself with every breath and blessing you.

10. We will now bring the meditation to a close. Rub your palms together and place them on your eyes. Gently rubbing your eyes with your fingers, open them.

Mystic Abilities

A dissertation on thought focus is incomplete without discussing siddhis (supernatural powers). Siddhis are material, paranormal powers, attained when the mind achieves a high level of concentration through yoga and meditation. These include telepathy (reading people's minds), clairvoyance (gaining information beyond the reach of ordinary senses) and psychokinesis (influencing matter by mind).

Sage Ved Vyas writes in the Bhagavatam:

aṇimā mahimā mūrter laghimā prāptir indriyaiḥ
prākāmyaṁ śhruta-dṛiṣhṭeṣhu śhakti-preraṇaṁ īśhitā

(11.15.4)

In this verse, Lord Krishna states that there are eight kinds of siddhis with the help of which material nature can be manipulated in a supernatural manner. In the next twenty verses, He explains that there are also ten minor siddhis. These comprise the power to know the past, present and future; tolerance of heat, cold and other dualities; the ability to see any distant thing; the power to make the body follow the mind wherever it goes; the ability to give up one's gross body and enter another's body through the pathways of the air, as easily as a bee leaves one flower and flies to another; the power to make the body free from injury, just as the bodies of aquatics are not injured by water.

However, in the thirty-third verse of the same chapter, Shree Krishna discourages the pursuit of all of them:

antarāyān vadanty tā yuṅjato yogam uttamam
mayā sampadyamānasya kāla-kṣhapaṇa-hetavaḥ

(11.15.33)

'These mystic perfections of yoga, which I have just mentioned, are actually impediments. They are a waste of time for those who practise the supreme yoga and wish to connect with Me.'

The Lord is the Supreme Mystic and the Master of all mystic perfections. To lose vision of Him and be drawn towards paranormal powers is like giving up a priceless jewel in exchange for broken pieces of glass.

Maharshi Patanjali, the writer of the *Yog Sutras*, is in full agreement with the above. In the third section of the scripture, *Vibhūti Pada*, he explains the very mystic perfections that are described in the Shreemad Bhagavatam. But then he states:

tadvairāgyādapi doṣhabījakṣhaye kaivalyam

(sutra 3.51)

'By giving up even these powers, the seed of evil is destroyed and liberation follows.'

In conclusion, it is a fact that developing the focus of the mind can lead to mystic abilities, if the aspirant seeks them. However, these are also viewed as distractions by those who have their eyes set on attaining the ultimate purpose of human life. With this understanding, let us continue our journey towards that supreme goal through the power of thoughts.

10

Creative Thinking—Your Hidden Treasure

People search the world for treasures without realizing the biggest gold mine exists within. Veritably, the ability to think well is the single biggest asset you can possess in life, if only you learn to manifest its potential by becoming a better thinker. Banks can fail, share markets can collapse and economies can regress, but in our thoughts, we possess a treasure chest that will never bottom out. No matter how dire the circumstances, this personal gold mine can provide us solutions and remedies, ideas and prospects.

Hence, our biggest and most reliable investment is the ability to think effectively. This treasure chest of thoughts is, in fact, the most accessible because it exists right between our ears. Yet, the paradox is that so few people discover and utilize it.

Why isn't every other person a thought leader, a creative writer or a visionary? Why are only a few people enriching themselves with their thoughts? The reason is that purposeful thinking is difficult. One of the best businessmen in Western history, Henry Ford, put it very well: 'Thinking is the hardest work there is, which is the probable reason why so few engage in it.'[1]

Ralph Waldo Emerson, the Age of Enlightenment philosopher from USA, posed a question and then answered it, 'What is the hardest task in the world? To think.'[2]

If anyone ever told you thinking is easy, do not believe them. They feel that way because they are reactive thinkers. However, focused creative thinking requires tremendous intellectual effort. So, let us learn how to think better.

Pause to Think

It is said: 'Experience is the best teacher.' But this statement is inaccurate. We learn from experiences only if we take the time to reflect. Else, they teach us

---

[1] 'Thinking is the Hardest Work There Is, Which Is Why So Few Engage In It', Quote Investigator, 5 April 2016, https://quoteinvestigator.com/2016/04/05

[2] Ralph Waldo Emerson Quotes, LibQuotes, https://libquotes.com/ralph-waldo-emerson/quote/lbs3g9s

nothing. That is why 'Evaluated experience is the best teacher.'

When we deliberately pause, we provide ourselves the leisure to reflect, learn and grow. Such deliberate pausing with intention enriches our thinking. Learning catches up with us and understanding dawns.

Most people put purposeful thinking on the back seat, while daily chores take precedence. However, without sufficient thought, they hurt themselves. A Sanskrit aphorism states: *avivekaḥ paramāpadām padam* 'When you act without thinking, you set yourself up for disaster.'

So, punctuate your day with pockets for thought and reflection. Before you rush into a meeting, schedule ten minutes to ponder about the implications and strategies. If you are a busy person, a great strategy is to block out time every day for just thinking. This is your 'sacred space' in terms of time.

Go beyond Popular Thinking

Mass thinking is easy; it is what the sheep do. I remember a riddle about sheep from childhood. This is how it goes:

Ten sheep were grazing by a railway track in the countryside. Five of them jumped on to the track and crossed over to the other side. How many were left behind?

That is simple. If five went to the other side, then five remained.

Wrong! The remaining sheep copied the others and also crossed over.

This is how sheep behave. While walking, they push their nose into the tail of the one ahead and walk. It is rare to see a sheep by itself. When it comes to thoughts, we tend to behave in a similar fashion.

We have no qualms about adopting others' thoughts because it saves us from the mental exertion of thinking ourselves. If we were requested to wear our neighbour's undergarments, how outraged we would be! But, in our head, we do not hesitate to blindly wear the ideas and perspectives of others. This paradigm of popular thinking prevents us from mining the gold mine of our own thought processes.

Most people adopt this option of majority thinking because it feels secure and safe. 'If the masses are doing it, then it must be right.'

A story is told of the British House of Commons. For seventy years, for a reason nobody seemed to know, an attendant would stand by the stairway. Everyone assumed that if he was standing there, it must be for a good reason.

Finally, someone decided to check on it. He discovered the job had been in the attendant's family for three generations. It had begun when the current attendant's grandfather was assigned the task of manning the spot. The stairway had just been painted and his job was to warn people about it. The paint had subsequently dried up, but not the job!

Unlike these parliamentarians was Copernicus. Popular thinking in the Western world said that the sun revolved around the earth. But Copernicus was willing to think beyond. With an open mind, he investigated celestial phenomena and mathematically proved that the earth revolved around the sun.

Galileo came soon after Copernicus. He too did not subscribe to conventional thinking. Two thousand years before him, Aristotle had said that heavier objects fall faster towards the earth. Hence, if two objects were taken to a great height and dropped, the heavier one would reach the earth first.

Aristotle's theory was incorrect, but everyone accepted it as an infallible truth. It only required one original thinker to try it practically. But two millennia went by after Aristotle, and nobody ever thought of questioning his statement until Galileo challenged it! His intention was to prove Copernicus' heliocentric theory of the universe. For that, he asserted that heaviness of objects had nothing to do with the speed of their fall (provided the air drag was negligible). Galileo gathered a crowd of scholars at the base of the Leaning Tower of Pisa. Then he went to the top and dropped two unequal weights; both landed at the same time.[3]

The scholars saw the evidence with their own eyes, yet they refused to believe it. They continued to assert that Aristotle could not be wrong. They were stuck in the trap of popular thinking. Fortunately for modern science, Copernicus and Galileo did not subscribe to the dictum, 'everyone thinks like this, so it must be right'. In fact, any scientist who made new discoveries could do so only by challenging the prevailing beliefs.

John Maynard Keynes, the economist whose ideas revolutionized how governments handled their economies, expressed it aptly. He said: 'The difficulty lies not so much in developing new ideas as in escaping from the old ones.'[4]

Four-Step Formula

Having realized the limitations of popular thinking, how do we go beyond? Here is a simple solution.

---

[3] Emily Conover, 'Galileo's Famous Gravity Experiment Holds Up, Even With Individual Atoms', Science News, 28 October 2020, https://www.sciencenews.org/article/galileo-gravity-experiment-atoms-general-relativity-einstein

[4] 'Quotations John Maynard Keynes', MacTutor School of Mathematics and Statistics, University of St. Andrews Scotland, Accessed August 2020, https://mathshistory.st-andrews.ac.uk/Biographies/Keynes/quotations/

Investigation

Pausing to think means more than just slowing down to smell the roses. It implies digging deeper for related information and knowledge. Rather than assuming that we know, we adopt a beginner's mindset. This means getting rid of the 'I already know' attitude.

An interesting episode highlighting the need for an investigative attitude is about the sale of Rolls-Royce Motors by its parent company, Vickers PLC, in 1998.[5]

The two customers were Volkswagen and BMW. Volkswagen won the bid to purchase the luxury car company for $780 million. However, after the sale was complete, the buyers made a shocking discovery. The rights to the use of the name 'Rolls-Royce' belonged to another company, Rolls-Royce PLC. The name was synonymous with luxury cars around the world. Without it, the purchase of the manufacturing facility, etc., would be of no use.

Even worse? The company that owned the name 'Rolls-Royce' had ties with BMW. Now, who do you think got to use the brand name? It was BMW and not Volkswagen.

---

[5] Alan Cowell, 'International Business; BMW To Get Rolls-Royce After All by Acquiring the Name', *The New York Times*, 29 July 1998, https://www.nytimes.com/1998/07/29/business/international-business-bmw-to-get-rolls-royce-after-all-by-acquiring-the-name.html

This was a case of poor investigation. The world is complex, and nobody understands it fully. If we develop fixed ideas, and become judgemental, prejudiced and biased, we block the learning process. Close-minded people are more interested in proving themselves right than in getting the best outcome. They do not ask questions and do not want their ideas challenged.

Instead, we must be open-minded to ideas from everywhere. The *Rig Veda* states: *ā no bhadrāḥ kratavo yantu viśhvataḥ* (mantra 1.89.1) 'Let noble thoughts come to us from all sides.'

Look at children. They are fascinated and curious about everything. When I have interactive sessions with children, they often pose the most unexpected questions. I remember a four-year-old asking me, 'What was Krishna's surname?'

I realized I had never thought about it before. Nor had any adult ever questioned me about Krishna's surname. But the little child's question got me thinking that the surnames of personalities are not mentioned in the Puranas, which means that the system of surnames did not exist in the past. How ironic to have a four-year-old open my eyes to this fact!

The investigative attitude means to be inquisitive and open-minded like a child. We never know from where a good idea may germinate.

The Dummies series of books have been a worldwide success.[6] *Initially, when the first few were launched in 1991, they met with resistance from booksellers, who thought that titles like 'Taxes for Dummies' would be insulting to customers, and nobody would be interested. To their surprise, however, the books were an unprecedented success. Today, there are over 3000 titles of the Dummies series in print, covering literally all topics of everyday life.*

Interestingly, the man behind the Dummies phenomenon, John Kilcullen, got the idea when he overheard a customer in a bookstore saying, 'Do you have a basic book about computers? Something like DOS for dummies?'

That helped Kilcullen perceive that the average reader is an intelligent person who feels dumb about a particular topic. Hence, the idea of books providing easy knowledge to fill the gap. He launched the Dummies series to help conquer fear associated with learning new topics.

The lesson here is to be open to information because it could come from an unexpected source or when we least expect it. Hence, the investigative stage in creative

---

[6] Jocelyn McClurg, 'The Genius of How-To Books for Dummies and Idiots', Hartford Courant, 12 May 1997, https://www.courant.com/news/connecticut/hc-xpm-1997-05-12-9705100053-story.html

thinking is like research, where you accumulate the intellectual resources from which you may be able to construct new ideas.

Incubation

After gathering the facts, do not expect your mind to come up with creative new ideas right away. Instead, let them simmer for a while in the cooker of your mind. This is the incubation stage.

Incubation is a subconscious process that is essential to creativity. It means letting the conscious mind rest and allowing the subconscious mind to get to work on the jigsaw puzzle. Overthinking with the conscious mind serves as a roadblock. Repeated experiments have proved that a short break does wonders for the creative process.

Henri Poincaré, in his essay 'Mathematical Creation' suggested that the best way to solve complex problems is to submerge yourself in the matter until you hit a wall.[7] Then, when you cannot go any further, distract yourself—preferably by taking a walk—and let the subconscious work on it. I can testify to the effectivity of the above technique from my own experience.

---

[7] Henri Poincaré, *Science and Method*, The University of Adelaide, 1913, Retrieved from https://ebooks.adelaide.edu.au/p/poincare/ henri/science-and-method/book1.3.html

It was the month of September in 2020 when I wrote this book. I must confess that every so often, I would have writer's block. I would be sitting before my laptop for an hour with no output. Now what to do? I would go out for a walk.

The weather in Dallas was perfect. And because of the pandemic, the streets were deserted; I could walk by myself on a practically empty street. In that calm and peace, I would revisit the topic on which I was stuck, and ideas would begin flowing. Upon returning to my room, I would put down 2000 words in a few hours.

This was my little experience with incubation. Lewis Carroll, author of *Alice in Wonderland*, called it 'mental mastication'. Alexander Graham Bell, inventor of the telephone, called it 'unconscious cerebration'.

Incubation can be done through a variety of activities, such as household chores, shaving, sipping a beverage, mowing the lawn, and so on. In fact, any activity that allows the conscious mind to rest can serve the purpose. Harper Lee (1926–2016), author of bestselling *To Kill A Mockingbird* and winner of the 1961 Pulitzer Prize, did much of her creative thinking while golfing.

Sleeping over a matter is another great way to incubate. Recent advances in neuroscience are providing evidence of how our brain consolidates the waking experiences into memory while we sleep.

Illumination

After incubation, bam! An idea will strike you in a flash of insight. This is the 'Eureka!' moment, when an intuitive realization happens, and you suddenly realize you know the answer.

What better example of it than the person who made 'Eureka' famous, Archimedes himself? He is remembered in history as the scientist who had an epiphany while soaking in his bathtub. He was so euphoric, he shouted 'Eureka! Eureka!' or 'I've found it! I've found it!' and ran naked through the streets of Syracuse in his excitement.

There are many such famous stories. For Newton, the moment of illumination came when the apple fell on his head. James Watt thought of inventing the steam engine while watching steam puffing out of a teapot on the stove.

Dmitri Mendeleev, the creator of the periodic table of elements, struggled to categorize the elements by their weight and fell asleep due to sheer exhaustion. He reported, 'I saw in a dream a table where all the elements fell into place as required. On waking up, I immediately wrote it down on a piece of paper. Only in one place did a correction seem necessary later.'[8]

---

[8] Adam Mellul, '150 Years On From Mendeleev's Periodic Table: Why it is Still A Work in Progress', The Oxford Student, 15 February 2019, https://www.oxfordstudent.com/2019/02/15/150-years-on-from-mendeleevs-periodic-table-why-it-is-still-a-work-in-progress/

Henri Poincaré, the mathematician we met a few paragraphs ago, worked on an equation for fifteen days without success. He decided to do something different. He drank black coffee because of which he could not sleep. So, he just sat in an easy chair and that was when the solution came to him. He says, 'Ideas rose in crowds; I felt them collide until pairs interlocked, so to speak, making stable combinations.

'By next morning I had established the existence of a class of Fuchsian functions, those which come from the hypergeometric series; I had only to write out the results which took but a few hours.'[9]

So, the message is clear: never skip incubation. Spend hours working on a problem, then switch off and let go. Hand it over to your subconscious. It is even possible that the Universe may step in on your side.

Since illumination does not come in words but in ideas, it invariably happens in a flash. Illumination cannot be an act of volition. The conscious mind can only welcome all the assembled elements floating suddenly into it. For example, Mozart would experience an entire piece of music in his head, not in linear progression, but all at one time.

---

[9] Henri Poincaré, *Science and Method*, The University of Adelaide, 1913, Retrieved from https://ebooks.adelaide.edu.au/p/poincare/henri/science-and-method/book1.3.html

Creative geniuses have often been convinced that their ideas came directly from God Himself. Hence, Mozart said, 'What I composed came to me so strongly, I could not forget. This is the best gift I have received from my Divine Maker.'[10]

Verification

Your intuition tells you the solution is found. But without verifying, you must not rashly accept it. The reason is that the intuition is not yet perfect and could be wrong. Hence, this is the stage when you take on the role of a scientist and validate the idea. If found unsatisfactory, you must then repeat the process from the beginning.

The verification stage also involves putting the inspiration into words, the vision into paint, and the idea into a business plan. Or simply, announcing it to the world.

So far, in this chapter, we have discussed the process of creative thinking. The previous chapter went into the depths of focused thinking. Let us now combine these two styles of thought.

---

[10] 'Mozart Bio Part 3', Russell Steinberg, 24 August 2011, http://www.russellsteinberg.com/blog/2013/9/26/mozart-bio-part-3

The Two Modes of Thinking

Salvador Dali was a famous surrealist painter in the last century. He was renowned for his precise draughtsmanship, technical skills and striking images. He also wrote fiction, poetry, essays and criticism.[11]

Dali's working style was seemingly strange. He would sit in an easy chair with a key in his hand. He would then let his brain wander freely until he fell asleep. He would wake up on hearing the sound of the key hitting the floor.

Then, he would immediately proceed to his study table and start jotting down in his notebook any ideas that were coming to him. He claimed that this was how he got the best ideas.

You may think this was eccentric behaviour. However, Salvador Dali was not alone in his working style.

The most successful inventor of all time, Thomas Edison, who has 1093 patents[12] *to his name in the US, had a similar style of thinking. He would think hard on a topic until he fell asleep. In a few moments, he would*

[11] Valeria Sabater, 'Salvador Dali's Method to Wake up our Creative Side', Exploring Your Mind, 15 November 2021, https://exploringyourmind.com/salvador-dalis-method-wake-creative-side/

[12] 'Thomas Edison Patents', Edison Innovation Foundation, https://www.thomasedison.org/edison-patents

wake up from his catnap and access the ideas coming to him.[13]

What was the rationale behind the thinking styles of these two? The answer is that our mind thinks in two modes—focused and diffuse. These illustrious thinkers were tapping into both the modes in their own idiosyncratic ways.

Let us understand these two modes of thinking. Compare them to a flashlight. We can adjust its settings to focus its beam. It will then light up one small area, but very brightly. Alternatively, we can change the setting to diffuse its beam. Then, it will illuminate a large area, but dimly.

Similarly, our mind also works in two modes. At times, it thinks in a diffuse way, allowing itself the luxury to wander freely. It makes connections with topics at random. In doing so, it uses the whole brain, without restricting itself to one area. This is creative thinking. It is also called **diffuse thinking** since it is the opposite of focused thinking.

In diffuse thinking, the conscious mind is relaxed. Our subconscious gets to work to link the ideas and

---

[13] 'Salvador Dali's Unusual Sleep Technique To Boost Creativity May Actually Work', IFLScience!, https://www.iflscience.com/brain/salvador-dals-unusual-sleep-technique-to-boost-creativity-may-actually-work/

concepts for you. As discussed in this chapter, diffuse thinking often happens while our conscious mind is engaged in some diversion, such as showering, walking or cooking. It is important to note that diffuse thinking works best when the task is physically engaging but we can do it without much thought. Then, the subconscious mind comes up with an important breakthrough. Here, we go wide but not deep.

However, getting a great idea is not the end. We need to follow it with **focused thinking**. In this kind of thinking, we engage our conscious mind in deep work to get tangible results. We are, therefore, focused, performing one task, while minimizing attention on everything else. Here, we go deep but not wide.

So, for example, if you are preparing a presentation for your company board, you have the information in your head. Your focus now is on putting it effectively into a PowerPoint presentation. At this time, you are thinking deliberately, with your conscious mind, to analyse problems and reach conclusions.

When we read a book, again our mind works in two modes. While reading, the intellect focuses on the particular sentence at hand. But every few paragraphs, the intellect steps back to develop the complete perspective of the text. Then again it focuses on the next sentence before it. That is the perennial rhythm of the mind—extracting information from the external world, withdrawing to reflect internally, and again returning to the outer realm.

On this topic, people frequently ask a question. Which is better—diffuse thinking or focused thinking? The answer is that both are necessary, just as eating and drinking are both necessary; it is pointless to ask which of the two is better. Likewise, to truly maximize our productivity, we must use both diffuse and focused thinking.

Having discussed creative and focused thinking, we will now learn about eight more styles of thought, to complete the decathlon.

11

The Decathlon of Thoughts

*T*he decathlon is the ultimate all-round event in track and field. It consists of ten different competitions conducted over two days. Conventionally, the winner of the decathlon receives the title of 'World's Greatest Athlete'. This tradition began with the Stockholm Olympics in 1912, when King Gustav V of Sweden told Jim Thorpe after he had just won the decathlon, 'You, sir, are the world's greatest athlete.'[1]

The first day's events are: 100-metre dash, running long jump, shot-put, high jump and 400-metre run. The 110-metre hurdles, discus throw, pole vault, javelin throw and 1500-metre run comprise the second day's events. Competitors receive scores for each event based on their performance, as per a table established by the International Association of Athletics Federations, recently renamed as World Athletics.

---

[1] Decathlon, Wikipedia, https://en.wikipedia.org/wiki/Decathlon

If all the present world records in the above events were a single athlete's scores in the decathlon, he would have gotten 12,568 points. As an individual athlete participating in all ten events over two days, Kevin Mayer holds the present world record of 9126 points.

Taking inspiration from the decathlon of athletics, let us consider a decathlon of thoughts. Have you come across people who are generalists, having a smattering of all kinds of knowledge, but they never go into the depths of any subject? They are examples of persons who have developed one mode of thought, general thinking, but are languishing in another mode— specialized thinking.

Our mind possesses the ability to engage in multiple modes of thought. In the previous chapter, we discussed focused thinking and diffuse thinking. It would, however, be a mistake to believe that these are the only two modes of thinking possible. In fact, the art of effective thinking is multifaceted; it includes a huge variety of thought skills. This is the decathlon of thoughts.

Big Picture Thinking

This is the mode of thinking to explore possibilities and identify opportunities amongst them. It requires looking at a problem from a broader perspective. The big picture perspective enables us to get a bird's-eye view of situations. And this, in turn, facilitates coming up with fresh ideas and new projects.

Big picture thinkers live at a 30,000 feet altitude, exploring opportunities and avenues for growth, thereby becoming visionaries in their field. However, being a visionary is not enough. The dream must be translated into an executable plan.

We must, therefore, pause from time to time to look up and around through big picture thinking. But then we must get into the nitty-gritty of details, schedules, project management, operational delivery, etc. This comes with the next kind of thinking.

Detail-Oriented Thinking

To do excellent work, we must get into the details by 'looking at the nuts and bolts', so to speak. The more detailed our planning, the better will be the execution.

When Maharshi Panini wished to write the rules of grammar for Sanskrit, he pondered over where he would feel inspired to do just that. Finally, he decided to proceed to Kailash and get guidance from Bhagavan Shankar.[2]

---

[2] Sanatanam Swaminathan, 'Lord Shiva and Panini, the Greatest Grammarian!', Speaking Tree, 17 Feb 2015, https://www. speakingtree.in/blog/lord-shiva-and-panini-the-greatest-grammarian?

As he reached the foot of the mountain, Lord Shiv, who was sitting atop Mount Kailash, saw the sage approaching. The omniscient Shivji understood Maharshi Panini's intention, and He thought, 'There is no need for him to climb all the way up. Let Me teach him from afar.'

This was probably the first recorded case of 'distance learning'. Lord Shiv played fourteen sounds on His damarū, which are famous today as Maheshwar Sutra:

a i u ṇ, ṛiḷ ṛi k, e o ṅ, ai au ch, ha ya va ra ṭ, la ṇ, ña ma ṅa ṇa na m,

jha bha ñ, gha ḍha dha ṣh, ja ba ga ḍa da śh, kha pha chha ṭha tha cha ṭa ta v,

ka pa y, śha ṣha sa r, ha l

The sage heard these sounds and understood what he had to do. He elaborated on them in his seminal work, Aṣhṭādhyāyī, *which contains eight chapters and 4000 aphorisms detailing the science of phonetics and grammar.*

The Aṣhṭādhyāyī *was the first complete text on grammar in any language of the world. However, it was still not detailed enough. It set the rules for Sanskrit grammar but did not explain them or give examples.*

Then, Katyayana wrote Vārttika, *wherein he reviewed Panini's work with the idea of explaining it. He added meanings of words and critical comments.*

Subsequently, another sage named Patanjali came along. He took the Aṣhṭādhyāyī *and* Vārttika *as the base and wrote his* Mahabhashya. *This became the reference book for the philosophy of grammar, and students go to it before trying to understand the other two works.*

In the historical examples above, Lord Shiv's *Maheshwar Sutra* is an example of big-picture thinking that was conveyed in a jiffy. Maharshi Panini's *Aṣhṭādhyāyī* is an example of detailed thinking as it required painstaking work. Yet, it did not suffice. Hence, *Vārttika* and *Mahabhashya* are examples of further detailed thinking.

Critical Thinking

This is the mode of thinking clearly and rationally to understand a matter in depth. The *Oxford Dictionary* defines critical thinking as 'the objective analysis and evaluation of an issue in order to form a judgement.'

Critical thinking relies on logical analysis instead of instinct. It is done objectively without allowing personal biases to colour the understanding. It is the opposite of 'everyday thinking', which is shallow, presumptive and not a candidate for the decathlon of thoughts.

Critical thinkers refuse to accept ideas and beliefs at face value. Instead, they are willing to question them rigorously. They seek to determine whether prevailing information and opinions represent the entire picture. And they are open to the possibility that the actuality may be different from what meets the eye.

The critical thinking skill is amongst the most sought-after skills in the workplace. With it, one can sift through information to distinguish between useful and useless detail to draw reasonable conclusions. Some examples are:

— An attorney has received a case. He analyses it to determine whether it is worth pursuing or if he should propose a settlement.

— A medical attendant analyses the cases at hand to determine their relative urgency. She then formulates the sequence in which they should be treated.

Reflective Thinking

People often share their devotional joys with me, saying things like, 'I loved my visit to Vrindavan', 'Today morning's meditation filled me with joy', 'Reading the Shreemad Bhagavatam was so insightful', etc.

I ask them, 'What was the part that you liked best?'

On hearing my question, the expression on their face changes. They start musing on their experience and bringing it back to their mind. It makes them savour the devotional bliss once again.

This is an example of reflective thinking, where we revisit past experiences to draw inspiration and learning from them. When we have a beautiful emotional experience, we love enjoying the thrill of it. However, in the heat of the moment, very rarely do we get a good perspective on it.

Reflective thinking allows us to revisit those good and bad experiences, and look upon them with fresh eyes, with the benefit of hindsight. The distance in time helps us develop dispassion and put things in proper perspective.

Reflective thinking is the reverse of 'attachment thinking', which is not included in the decathlon of thoughts. Attachment thinking is where our emotions prevent us from seeing things as they are. As the saying goes, 'love is blind'. As a matter of fact, 'hate is also blind'. In both cases, the attachment of the intellect prevents us from assessing the situation objectively. And this limits our understanding. The value of reflective thinking is that it takes experiences and converts them into learning.

You may have come across advertisements for jobs mentioning eligibility criteria such as 'five years of work experience necessary'. Why such a precondition? The reason is that an educational degree is no guarantee of proficiency. One learns many insights only through experience. That learning is made possible by reflection.

Mark Twain put it very well: 'We should be careful to get out of an experience all the wisdom that is in it—and stop there; lest we be like the cat that sits down on a hot stove-lid. She will never sit down on a hot stove-lid again—and that is well; but also she will never sit down on a cold one anymore.'[3]

Strategic Thinking

It is another name for 'planning'. Its aim is to devise an effective blueprint for action. Hence, it is the bridge between where you are today and where you wish to be tomorrow. The goal of strategic thinking is to take complex long-term objectives and break them down into simpler goals.

Chandragupta Maurya was one of the greatest kings to rule India in the last 2500 years. He lived during the time of Alexander's arrival in India. Alexander installed several administrators in various kingdoms

---

[3] 'Mark Twain: Quotes', Britannica, Accessed September 2020, https://www.britannica.com/quotes/Mark-Twain

before he left for Greece. The most powerful of them was Seleucus Nicator, who governed large portions of India.

Under the guidance of his guru, the famous Chanakya, Chandragupta was on a mission to recover India's territories from its Greek administrators. Legend has it that at one point, he was losing badly, so he fled. He disguised himself to avoid being recognized and travelled through the lesser-known villages.

He reached the home of an old woman and begged for food. She offered him hot khichdi on banana leaves. When Chandragupta tried to eat it, his fingers got burnt and he screamed in pain.

The old woman remarked, 'You are as foolish as our emperor, Chandragupta. You are eating the khichdi from the centre instead of starting at the edge. Chandragupta too is trying to take on the entire Greek army at one time.'

It is said that Chandragupta got the message and changed his strategy. He engaged in strategic thinking. He began annexing small portions of the kingdom until he grew strong enough. Later, he defeated the Macedonian satrapies in the north-west of the Indian subcontinent. He then went on to wage a war against Seleucus, who accepted defeat and gave his daughter's hand in marriage to Chandragupta. With Seleucus' help, Chandragupta established the biggest empire in all Asia in his time, second in the world only to Alexander's.

Abstract Thinking

This is the mode of thinking beyond the 'here and now'. In it, we seek to understand how the subject of our thought relates to everything else. We do not just ask how; we also ask why. We look for deeper meanings and underlying patterns in things.

Some examples of abstract thinking are thinking about intangible concepts, such as freedom and equality. Using our imagination to ponder about possibilities and options. Creating relationships between ideas, and so on.

Those who are good abstract thinkers can perceive analogies and relationships that others cannot. Thereby, they can lift their wisdom to higher levels of insight. However, mere ideas that never get implemented serve no purpose. These must be translated into tangible results with the help of the next mode of thinking.

Practical Thinking

This is the use of common sense to evaluate the feasibility of ideas. It utilizes good judgement to make decisions that will produce results. It eliminates excessive ideas that waste time and helps us focus on what really counts.

Practical persons focus on carrying out productive actions. They prioritize tangible outputs and beneficial goals. They value processes, but only to the extent that they bring results.

It may seem that practical persons do not have fancy ideas, but this is not the case. For them, concrete results are simply more worthwhile than ideas or intentions. They are wary of ideas that are mere talk and never translate into action.

Practical thinkers are realists. They easily capture the essentials of any situation or person. They focus on what is important and avoid beating around the bush. As the saying goes, they have their 'feet firmly on the ground'. They know how to prioritize their work into hierarchies of importance and stick to their priorities. Practical thinking plays a vital role, particularly in crisis situations, where theorizing does not count for much.

Mature Thinking

As humans, we are emotional creatures, and our brain is hardwired for sentiments. Every thought that crosses our head creates feelings. These lead to emotions of lesser or greater intensity. To be good thinkers, we are required to master our sentiments. The head and the heart need to work together in alignment.

Being a book-smart intellectual does not necessarily imply that we also possess emotional maturity. In fact, many intelligent people are unable to manage their own feelings. Further, they are inept at empathizing with the feelings of others, and hence difficult to work with. Their emotional immaturity gets in the way of being effective in real-life situations.

The reverse of this is mature thinking. It includes three components:

Emotional Self-Awareness

The first step in becoming a mature person is awareness of our own emotions. Without it, there can be no scope for managing them. For example, if we do not even know we are suffering from foul anger, there will be no scope for overcoming it.

Emotional Self-Management

It is the ability to alter our emotions without needing the environment to change. It is practically undeveloped in childhood. Hence, when children are in a bad mood, they blame others for their own feelings. They have not yet learnt to control their emotions. But as we grow up, we are expected to take responsibility for our sentiments and stop pointing fingers at others.

Emotionally mature are those who know how to be happy, inspired and optimistic. They do not get angry in stressful situations and can calmly focus on solutions. They can be relied upon because they do not make rushed emotional decisions.

Emotional Empathy

This implies awareness of the needs and feelings of others. Empathetic people are good at managing relationships, paying attention to the non-verbal communication of others and relating to them. They avoid jumping to judgements or stereotyping others.

Mature people have the ability to see things from the viewpoint of others. This prevents them from blindly supporting their own opinion. Consequently, they are better at diplomatically resolving conflicts and at managing change.

In the previous two chapters, we discussed focused thinking and creative thinking. The present chapter has covered eight further modes of thinking. With this, the decathlon of thoughts is now complete:

1. Creative thinking

2. Focused thinking

3. Big picture thinking

4. Detail-oriented thinking

5. Critical thinking

6. Reflective thinking

7. Strategic thinking

8. Abstract thinking

9. Practical thinking

10. Mature thinking

Good thinkers are those who can use any or all of these styles depending upon the situation at hand. This enables them to work effectively in the world and produce valuable results. Senior executives in any corporate organization are expected to possess all these thinking skills, as that is what they are paid for.

Beyond professional success, however, we must also make our personal life a success. For this, we must learn another thinking skill. Let us discuss it next.

12

Spiritual Thinking

The progress of science has bestowed powerful technologies on humankind. Through genetic engineering, we can modify plant species and create Genetically Modified Organisms (GMOs). We know how to create designer babies through genome editing and in vitro fertilization. And we can split the plutonium atom to manifest nuclear energy. But we are now stumped by ethical issues regarding what is right and what is wrong and where to draw the line.

Science cannot answer these questions for us because it does not possess values. It can put nuclear power in our hands, but it cannot tell us about the right or wrong use of that power. This is why the progress of scientific knowledge has been accompanied by global warming, rampant pollution and depletion of the ozone layer. We now have new problems in the form of over-urbanization and rapid diminution of mineral wealth and non-renewable energy resources.

If wisdom comes from knowledge, then why can scientific knowledge not resolve the ethical dilemmas surrounding its usage? Because they are beyond the purview of material science. To understand ethics and morality, we must turn to another branch of knowledge, which is spiritual science. The *Atharva Veda* states:

> *dve vidye veditavye iti ha*
> *sma yad-brahmavido vadanti, parā chaivāparā cha*
> (*Muṇḍakopaniṣhad* 1.1.4)

'There are two kinds of knowledge that we must cultivate—material knowledge and spiritual knowledge. The knowers of Brahman have said this.'

Having discussed material thinking in depth in the last few chapters, we will now proceed to understand spiritual thinking.

Why We Need Spirituality

Emotional mastery is a wonderful thing for it helps us feel in control of ourselves. The decathlon of thoughts is also great because it empowers us to become effective thinkers. But the big questions in life still remain unanswered. What is the ultimate purpose of my life? Who am I? Why have I come to this world? And what are my duties in life?

If we do not know the answers to these questions, then we are simply running around like a chicken with its head cutoff, not knowing even the goal of life. We may master all the styles of thinking, but without spiritual thinking they have no ultimate value; they are like a bunch of zeros without a number in front.

Our soul yearns to connect with something sacred and higher than us. To go beyond the everyday grind of mundane existence. To find a deeper purpose to life. The reason is that we are not material beings having a spiritual experience. Rather, we are spiritual beings having a material experience in this world of maya. This is why our humdrum day-to-day experiences do not fulfil us. The thirst for spiritual nourishment becomes so intense for some that they renounce everything else in pursuit of it. We are all familiar with the example of the Buddha.

Siddharth was born in a royal family, in the midst of immense worldly opulence.[1] *But at the time of his birth, astrologers warned his parents not to let him see the reality of life.*

His parents took all precautions. Growing up, they did not allow him to go outside the palace walls. They even got him married to a beautiful princess, named

[1] Joshua Mark, 'Siddhartha Gautama', World History Encyclopedia, 23 September 2020, https://www.worldhistory.org/Siddhartha_Gautama/

Yashodhara, with whom he had an angelic little child, named Rahul.

Then one day, Siddharth went on a tour of his kingdom and saw a sick man, an old man and a corpse. It set Siddharth thinking, 'This is the reality of life. One day, I will also fall sick, grow old and die. Then what is the purpose of life? I must find out.'

We all know that Siddharth renounced the world in search of answers. After achieving enlightenment, he became known as the Buddha.

The Buddha was not the only one to experience such a strong call for spirituality that he renounced the world. History is testimony to Adi Shankaracharya, Nimbarkacharya, Ramanujacharya, Madhvacharya, Chaitanya Mahaprabhu and millions of other ascetics, sadhus and sanyasis who have followed this path.

However, spirituality does not require us to renounce the world. In fact, the Bhagavad Gita informs us that it can be practised at home as well:

sannyāsaḥ karma-yogaśh cha niḥshreyasa-karāvubhau
tayos tu karma-sannyāsāt karma-yogo viśhiṣhyate

(verse 5.2)

In this verse, Lord Krishna explains that one can be spiritual both as a sanyasi (renunciant monk) and as a *grihastha* (householder). But practising spirituality while living in household life is even more praiseworthy than renunciation.

Having understood its importance, let us get to the bottom of what spiritual thinking is.

Difference between Religion and Spirituality

As I travel around the world giving discourses, I am often asked the question: 'What is the difference between religion and spirituality?'

The difference is that spirituality is the essence, while religion is its external form. For example:

- Going on the *Char Dham Yatra* to visit the four sacred places is religion. To sit down in one place and take our mind to the Divine is spirituality.

- To take a bath in the holy Ganga is religion. To bathe our mind in divine thoughts is spirituality.

- To adorn the body with sacred tilak marks is religion. To adorn our personality with noble and sublime qualities is spirituality.

- To offer oblations of ghee in the sacrificial fire is religion. To offer our obnoxious ego at the feet of God and become humble is spirituality.

Religion will please your grandmother and make you look holy in the eyes of society. Spirituality will please God and make you holy from within.

But that does not mean religion is a waste of time. Nowadays, many teenagers and young adults reject religious practices on the pretext of being spiritual. They do not want to have anything to do with poojas. They ridicule their parents and the older generations for indulgence in religious practices. When asked whether they visit temples, they say they are practising spirituality. While the reality is that they become slaves of their whimsical mind and do nothing, neither spiritual nor religious.

The truth is that without the help of any external rituals, the practise of spirituality is exceedingly difficult because the mind does not get the support it requires for nurturing divine thoughts. Hence, in the initial stages of the spiritual journey, the external rituals are immensely beneficial. This is why the scriptures and saints have created systems of traditions, customs and ceremonies. These are the religious practices that get passed down from generation to generation.

At the same time, the scriptures also warn that we must not remain stuck in the rituals. Rather, we must strive to reach their goal, which is to purify our mind and think of God.

If we only practise external holiness and forget the essence, they are again a bunch of zeros without the one in front. Thus, Sage Ved Vyas writes:

dharmaḥ svanuṣhṭhitaḥ puṁsāṁ
  viṣhvaksena-kathāsu yaḥ
notpādayed yadi ratiṁ
  śhrama eva hi kevalam (Bhagavatam 1.2.8)

'You may perfectly follow the external form of religions, but if it does not result in attachment to the lotus feet of Lord Krishna, it is mere waste of time.'

Similarly, Saint Kabir has condemned the practise of empty rituals with such strong words:

pothī paḍhi paḍhi jag muā, paṅḍit bhayā na koy
ḍhāī ākṣhar prem ke, paḍhe so paṅḍit hoy

'Reading the scriptures, the whole world died, and nobody became a pandit. But if anyone can learn these two and a half syllables, *Prem* (love), that person will be the true pandit.'

Like Saint Kabir, hundreds of bhakti saints who came 500 years ago inspired the masses to go to the essence of religious practices, which is spirituality. Taking inspiration from them, let us study how we can become more spiritual.

Four Aspects of Spiritual Thinking

Simply put, spirituality has four components to it.

Self-Awareness Skills

These include:

1. Distinguishing our lower nature from our higher nature.

2. Awareness of the purpose of our life.

3. Awareness of the values we live by.

If our knowledge of the 'self' is itself incorrect, then our self-analysis and self-goals will also be erroneous. That is why the answer to 'Who am I?' is the foundation of spiritual thinking.

There is a joke about the Greek philosopher, Socrates. He was in the habit of asking his disciples to ponder deeply about the self. It is said that once he was walking down a street in Greece. Absorbed in deep thought, he absent-mindedly bumped into a policeman.

The incensed policeman said, 'What a strange fellow you are! Can you not see where you are going? Who are you?'

Socrates responded with glee, 'Sir, I have been wondering about who I am for the last forty years. If you have any idea, please let me know.'

To answer the question, 'Who am I?' modern psychology presents the concept of the **Johari window**. It states that there are four perceptions of the 'self'.

These are the known self, the hidden self, the blind self and the unknown self.[2]

1. **The known self** is what you and others know about yourself. This is the aspect of your personality that you can freely discuss with others.

2. **The hidden self** is what you know and see in yourself, but others do not. This is your privacy, which you do not disclose to the public. Possibly, you are embarrassed about these areas. Or else, you feel that disclosing your faults and weaknesses will make you vulnerable.

3. **The blind self** is what you do not see in yourself, but others do. For example, you may feel you are gentle and kind in your dealings. But if you ask your friends, they may feel you are inconsiderate and aggressive.

4. **The unknown self** is the aspect of your personality that neither you nor others can see. This may include untapped potential and talents that have not yet been identified and explored.

Such an analysis helps us understand our self-identity. However, the question, 'Who am I?' remains unanswered.

---

[2] Peter Omondi, 'The Johari Window Model', Communication Theory, 30 October 2021, https://www.communicationtheory.org/the-johari-window-model/

Greater clarity on this question comes from the Vedic scriptures. They explain that our body cannot be the basis of our self-identity. The body constantly changes from infancy to adulthood to old age. And yet, we remain the same person. If we were the body, we too would keep changing along with it. Hence, we are not the body.

Likewise, we are not the mind and intellect either, for these keep changing too. Beyond all these is the soul, which is divine and non-material. Lord Krishna explains in the Bhagavad Gita: 'The souls in this material world are My eternal fragmental parts. But bound by material nature, they are struggling with the six senses, including the mind.' (verse 15.7)

The soul is also referred to as *jīva*, atma, spirit, *noor*, etc., in various religious traditions. Self-awareness based on our identity as divine souls is the first skill in spiritual thinking. Now, let us move on to the second.

Universal Awareness Skills

This is the wisdom to see the connection between ourselves and the Universe. It includes awareness of the interconnectedness of all creation.

The recent pandemic has revealed how interrelated the world is. A microscopic virus that emerged in one country rapidly affected the entire planet. Similarly, excessive release of carbon dioxide in one continent results in global warming that impacts all continents. Likewise, wiping out forests brings its consequences in the form of climate change.

In fact, biologists have realized how sensitive the ecology of any place is. All creatures in the food chain have a role to play. Eliminating even one species brings about a chain reaction that disrupts the entire environment.

Universal awareness skills include:

1. Empathy for the opinions and views of others.

2. Awareness of the interconnectedness of the Universe.

3. Awareness of the spiritual laws that govern the Universe.

Vedic knowledge makes incorporating these in our thinking quite easy. Shree Krishna states in the Bhagavad Gita: 'I am the origin of all creation. Everything proceeds from Me.' (verse 10.8)

When we see all of creation is connected to its source, who is God, we naturally develop universal awareness, the second skill in spiritual thinking.

Self-Mastery Skills

It is the ability to put spiritual knowledge into practice in personal and professional life. It is the practical implementation of theoretical knowledge.

A couple's eighteen-year-old son died. This plunged them into a veritable ocean of grief. Nevertheless, rituals had to be performed for his cremation. For that purpose, they called a pandit.

As was the tradition, the pandit gave a lecture from the second chapter of the Bhagavad Gita. He explained that the soul is immortal, and hence, nobody dies. There is no reason for grief. Hearing the pandit's wise words, the parents nodded in agreement. 'Yes, Panditji! You are right. We should not cry.'

Fifteen days went by and the pandit's goat died. Now, he began wailing in grief, 'My goat has died! My goat has died.'

The parents came to know of his sorrow and asked him, 'Panditji, earlier when our son died, you explained to us that to grieve is ignorance. Now your goat is dead and you are crying?'

The pandit replied, 'Yes, I did advise you not to cry. But the child was yours, and the goat was mine. I was attached to it.'

The pandit did have spiritual knowledge but was not able to live by it. Hence, the third set of skills in spiritual thinking includes:

1. Commitment to keeping our higher self in charge.

2. Living according to our values and purpose.

3. Commitment to pursuing our spiritual growth.

These virtues are the bedrock for leading a life aligned with our higher values. These require sustained motivation, self-discipline and determination. They enable us to develop self-mastery skills, the third skill in spiritual thinking.

Professional Mastery Skills

This is our ability to make a positive difference in the lives of others. Mohammed Ali put it very beautifully: 'Service to others is the rent you pay for your room here on earth.'[3]

Some people view life as an ice-cream cone—you have one chance to enjoy it before it finishes. In contrast, spiritual thinking means viewing life as a candle. The goal is to serve to your fullest extent before life gets extinguished.

Let us learn from a delightful story how serving others leads to joy and peace.

A wealthy old woman lived in great opulence. She possessed all the luxuries and comforts that people work hard for, but she still felt miserable. She could not understand what was missing in her life.

The woman went to a psychologist and asked him, 'Sir, God has blessed me with so much. I can fulfil any

---

[3] 'Muhammad Ali Hand Wrote "Service to Others Quote" – Atlanta Hilton', http://seve-astorg-us7h.squarespace.com/speci/muhammad-ali-hand-wrote-letter-atlanta-hilton

desire that arises in my mind, but why does happiness elude me? And why do I feel so miserable?'

Outside the doctor's chamber, a sweeper was mopping the floor. The psychologist said to the woman, 'I always see a beaming smile on this sweeper's face. Let us ask him the secret of his happiness.'

He called the sweeper and posed the question to him. The sweeper replied, 'Sir, two years ago, my wife of thirty years died of breast cancer. I was heartbroken. The very next month, my only son died in a car crash. My grief knew no end. I did not know what to do with myself and how to handle my depression.

'One day, I had gone to the market to purchase vegetables. While returning, a cat started following me. On reaching home, I opened the door and went in. The cat continued to stand on my doorstep in hunger and anticipation. Moved to compassion, I brought milk for it in a saucer. The cat lapped up all the milk from the saucer. Then it did something I did not expect. It began purring with affection and rubbing itself against my leg.

'For the first time in many months, I broke into a smile. Then I began thinking that if helping a little cat gave me so much happiness, then why not help my neighbours as well? I knew of an old woman in the neighbourhood who was bedridden. I baked a cake and *took it to her. As I began serving people with whatever little I had, I experienced deep happiness within my soul. I have made that the goal of my life, and it is the secret of the joy I experience.'*

The joy our soul is yearning for does not come from gratifying the desires of our mind and senses. It comes by using our talents and skills in the service of others, and for the pleasure of God.

Hence, the fourth aspect of spiritual thinking is social and professional mastery skills. These include:

1. Serving through your professional work.

2. Serving in your personal relationships.

3. Serving through your position of leadership.

It is said there are three stages in life: learn, earn and return. First, we undergo education to acquire skills and competencies. Second, we begin working to earn and take care of ourselves. And third, we use our abilities and possessions to give back to the world.

In this chapter, we discussed how spiritual thinking provides meaning and purpose to all the different aspects of our life. When spiritual intelligence begins to blossom, it brings the realization that we are not cut off from the Universe. Rather, we are fragments of God, and our dharma as His little parts is to serve Him.

In serving with our talents and abilities, we receive the fulfilment that our soul is yearning for.

There is one final mode of thinking, which is divine thinking. These are thoughts imbued with pure loving devotion.

13

Divine Thinking

In the last chapter we discussed spiritual thinking, which provides meaning and purpose to life. It fulfils the thirst of our soul to connect our lives with the sacred. However, divine thinking goes even further; it imbues our every thought with selfless love, or bhakti.

Divine thinking is so powerful that it enchants even the Supreme Almighty. That is why in the Shreemad Bhagavatam, Lord Krishna states:

> My pure devotees are free from personal desire and deeply absorbed in loving devotion to Me. They are devoid of enmity and equally disposed to all. I walk behind the devotees who have reached such an exalted state so that I may get the dust of their lotus feet and be purified.
>
> (11.14.16)

Imagine the glory of devotion! We all know that God is *pāvanaṁ pāvanānām* (the source of all purity in the world). Yet, the same Lord feels so enraptured by His devotees that He wishes to gather the dust of their feet to purify Himself.

In this chapter, we will discuss how to lift our thoughts to that sublime level through devotion. First, let us develop appreciation for divine love and then we will get into the methodology for practising it.

The Miraculous Power of Bhakti

Vidyapati (1352–1448 AD) was an elevated poet-saint[1]. He is often called 'Maithil Kavi Kokil', (the Poet Cuckoo Saint of Mithila). He influenced the development of many east Indian languages, such as Maithili, Bhojpuri, Bengali and Odia. He was a fervent devotee of Lord Shiv.

Enthralled by Vidyapati's devotion, Lord Shiv disguised himself as a servant and went to him. He introduced Himself as 'Ugna' and requested the saint to employ Him. Vidyapati employed Lord Shiv, in the form of Ugna, who became an affectionate servant to the poet-saint.

One day, Vidyapati received an invitation from the king of Mithila. He undertook the journey with Ugna.

---

[1] Abhishek Jha, 'Bhakta, Bhagwan, and MahaShivaratri', The Seer, 27 February 2017, https://theseer.in/bhakta-bhagwan-and-mahashivaratri/

On the way, Vidyapati felt very thirsty but there was no water around. Concerned for him, Lord Shiv took the water of the Ganga, which always resides in the locks of His hair, and gave it to Vidyapati to drink.

On sipping the water, Vidyapati realized that this was no ordinary water, rather, it was the sacred Ganga jal. He insisted on knowing how Ugna had procured the holy water in that arid place. Left with no option, Ugna revealed His original form as Gangeshwar, Lord Shiv.

Vidyapati felt deeply sorry that he had unknowingly engaged his Ishta Dev (worshipped Lord) in his service. But Lord Shiv pacified him by saying that it was His own desire. He continued living with Vidyapati on the condition that poet-saint would not divulge His original identity to anyone.

But how could Vidyapati now avail services from Ugna after discovering His identity? Instead, Vidyapati would keep planning for his Ishta Dev's comfort. On seeing this, Vidyapati's wife would get incensed. She would wonder what was wrong with her husband. One day, she got annoyed with Ugna for a trivial reason and began beating Him with a broom. Her husband, knowing Ugna's true identity, could not tolerate this and blurted out, 'What are you doing! He is Lord Shiv Himself.'

Vidyapati realized his mistake but it was too late. The condition for Lord Shiv's to live there had been broken and He immediately vanished. The poet-saint then searched for his Ugna in forests, in the countryside and in temples. Finally, in a place known today as Ugnasthan, Lord Shiv gave him darshan and then asked him to continue with his life's mission of propagating the glories of pure devotion.

What a mind-boggling story! The Master of the universe became the servant of His devotee. And this was not just a one-of-a-kind occurrence. Indian history is full of hundreds of such stories where devotees enslaved God by the power of their love.

The scriptures too repeatedly sing the glories of *nishkām* bhakti (selfless devotion). In the Bhagavatam, the Lord declares:

ahaṁ bhakta-parādhīno hy asvatantra iva dvija
sādhubhir grasta-hṛidayo bhaktair bhakta-jana-priyaḥ

(9.4.63)

'I get enslaved by those devotees who love Me selflessly, free from material desires. I do not remain independent, for they capture My heart. What to speak of them, even the devotees of My devotees are exceedingly dear to Me.'

At this point, we may ask, 'What is the nature of this entity called bhakti that enslaves God?' The next section provides the answer.

What is Bhakti?

Here are some of the ways in which bhakti has been defined by the saints and scriptures. I am excluding the Sanskrit verses for an easy read:

'To absorb the mind in God and relish His divine bliss is bhakti.'

—Gopal Tapaniya Upanishad

'Just as the holy Ganga flows incessantly towards the ocean, similarly, when our thoughts begin to flow towards God, that divine state is called bhakti.'

—Shreemad Bhagavatam 3.29.11

'If needles are inserted into a potato, they remain lodged in it. Likewise, if all our thoughts are anchored in God, that state is called bhakti.'

—Jagadguru Shankaracharya

'Meditation that is endowed with love for God is bhakti.'

—Jagadguru Ramanujacharya

'The word "bhakti" has come from the etymological root "bhaj", which means "to serve". Hence, bhakti is service to the Lord.'

—Sage Ved Vyas

Jagadguru Kripaluji Maharaj accepts all the above definitions. But he further elaborates that bhakti is a divine power. The highest power of God is *Yogmaya*. The essence of *Yogmaya* is *Hlādinī* shakti, the power that gives pleasure to God. The quintessence of *Hlādinī* shakti is Prem shakti, or divine love.

In conclusion, the bhakti we wish to possess is a divine energy, a shakti of God.

The Way to Get Bhakti

Million-dollar question: 'How can we get divine love for God?'

Answer: It cannot develop through any spiritual practice you may do. The *Bhakti Rasamrit Sindhu* states: 'We may do millions of sadhanas for countless ages, yet they will not result in divine love.'

Bhakti is not like a seed that you sow and nurture it into a plant one day. **Divine love is a shakti of God. It is received by the soul through God's grace that comes through the Guru.**

Question: If devotion is received by grace, then why is it given to some and not to others?

Answer: There is a condition for bestowing it. God and Guru say, 'We are eager to give it to you, but you do not have a suitable vessel to receive it. Bring a proper vessel and we will give it to you.' The vessel here refers to the ethereal heart, where bhakti must reside.

A disciple went to his guru and requested, 'Guruji, please give me five litres of milk.'

'How can I give it, my child, unless you have a vessel to hold it?' replied the guru.

The next time, the disciple returned with a pot. 'Guruji, I have a vessel now. Please give me the milk.'

'Son, your vessel has holes in it. The milk will leak. Get a vessel that will not leak,' instructed the guru.

The disciple went away and returned with a leakproof pot. 'Guruji,' he said, 'Now, please grant me the milk.'

'My child,' responded the guru again, 'Your vessel does not have holes, but it is dirty. The milk will ferment if I pour in it. Get a clean vessel.'

Likewise, divine love is such a sublime power that it can only reside in a pure heart.

Question: How can we purify and prepare the vessel of our heart?

Answer: For that, we will need to do another form of bhakti, called *sadhana bhakti*. Jagadguru Shree Kripaluji Maharaj explains in *Bhakti Śhatak*:

pratham sādhanā bhakti karu, tab man nirmal hoy
milai viśhuddhā bhakti tab, guru anukaṁpā toy

(verse 9)

'First, do *sadhana bhakti* and purify your mind. Then you will receive divine love by the grace of the guru.'

There are, hence, two types of bhakti—one that we must practise and one that we will receive:

- **The bhakti we must practise is called** *sadhana bhakti*, or preparatory devotion.

- **The bhakti we receive through grace is called** *siddha bhakti*, or perfect devotion.

Siddha bhakti is the divine love energy we talked about, which is the quintessence of *Yogmaya shakti*. It will be bestowed by the Guru when the vessel of our heart is ready.

Sadhana bhakti is preparatory devotion that we must practise to purify our heart. The next section explains how it is to be practised.

How to do Sadhana Bhakti

To cleanse the mind through preparatory devotion, we must fulfil three requirements:

> *hari guru bhaju nit govind rādhey*
> *bhāv nishkām ananya banā de*
> > (*Radha Govind Geet* verse 53)

The three conditions of *sadhana bhakti*, as explained by Jagadguru Kripaluji Maharaj in the above verse, are *ananya bhakti, nirantar bhakti* and *niṣhkām bhakti.* Let us learn about each of them.

Ananya Bhakti (Exclusive Devotion)

Compare the mind to a cloth which has not been cleaned for a long time and is thus very dirty. The dirt will be removed by washing the cloth with clean water. Since the dirt is excessive, the cloth will have to be washed multiple times. But the condition is that the water must be clean. If the water itself is dirty, then the cloth will only become more unclean.

Similarly, the Supreme Divine Personality is all-pure. When we attach our mind to Him, it gets cleansed. But if, alongside, we allow worldly affection or hatred to persist, the purification cannot happen. **Ananya bhakti is devotion where the mind is attached exclusively to God, and nowhere else in the world.** We must live in the world but not let the world live in us. Just as a boat is in the water, but the water is not in the boat. This is the first condition of *sadhana bhakti.*

The Bhagavad Gita emphasizes *ananya bhakti*:

ananya-chetāḥ satataṁ yo māṁ smarati nityaśhaḥ
tasyāhaṁ sulabhaḥ pārtha nitya-yuktasya yoginaḥ

(verse 8.14)

'For those yogis who always think of Me with exclusive devotion, I am easily attainable because of their constant absorption in Me.'

Nitya Bhakti (Continuous Devotion)

The second condition of *sadhana bhakti* is to practise the presence of God at all times.

In the olden days, when there were no matchsticks, people would use firewood to light a fire.[2] *They would rub two pieces of firewood together and ignite them. But the condition was that they had to be rubbed together for a sufficient amount of time without a break. If they were rubbed for five minutes and stopped, then again rubbed for five minutes and again stopped, the wood would wear away but not ignite. The temperature had to keep increasing continuously in order to light the fire.*

The mind can also be likened to firewood. Our remembrance of God must be without a break for divine grace to manifest. Hence, the Bhagavad Gita repeatedly stresses continuous remembrance:

> *tasmāt sarveshu kāleshu mām anusmara*   (8.7)
> *satataṁ kīrtayanto māṁ*   (9.14)
> *nitya-yuktā upāsate*   (12.2)
> *mām ekaṁ śharaṇaṁ vraja*   (18.66)

---

[2] Ljiljana Djuriĉic̀ 'Ancient Methods of Making Fire', Accessed August 2020, https://core.ac.uk/download/pdf/225623231.pdf

All these verses state that our mind must constantly remain in God.

Question: How can we perform our worldly tasks if we are to always remember God?

Answer: This can be done by constantly realizing the presence of God. While going about our worldly duties, we must perceive that God is with us, as our Witness and Protector. Thus, our consciousness will remain linked to Him. And we can do our works for His pleasure, as an offering to the Divine.

Niṣhkām Bhakti (Selfless Devotion)

This is the third condition for sadhana bhakti. Our devotion must not be motivated by self-seeking. **True love is that where we are willing to give our all and seek nothing in return.**

If we worship God and in return ask for worldly gains, then it does not remain love; it becomes a form of business. 'O God, I will love you, but You must do this work for me.' This is not love; it is a transaction.

Why does love fade so quickly in the world, and why do lovers keep quarrelling with each other? The reason is that worldly love is selfish. Both lovers are focused on their own happiness.

Divine love is the reverse. The *Narad Bhakti Darshan* describes it as: *tat sukh sukhitvam* (sutra

24). 'The goal of divine love is the happiness of the Beloved.'

We have briefly discussed the three conditions for sadhana bhakti. Now let us move on and see what happens when we practise such devotion.

Sadhana Bhakti Purifies Our Thoughts

The result of bhakti is that our mind gets cleansed and imbued with God-consciousness. This changes the nature of our thoughts. In such a devotional state, the devotee sees God in everyone like the sadhu in the following story.

A farm worker was toiling in a paddy field when the landowner came along. They had an altercation, which made the landowner furious, and he began beating the worker with a stick.

A sadhu was standing nearby. He was moved to compassion and chided the landowner for beating the poor man. Now the landowner became annoyed with the sadhu and used his stick upon him. He beat him so severely that the poor sadhu fainted.

Other villagers from nearby came rushing to help the sadhu. They carried him to the hospital, where he was taken care of. When the sadhu recovered consciousness, the villagers who had brought him to the hospital enquired, 'Who beat you so badly?'

'Ram,' said the sadhu.

'Ram? Which Ram?' asked the villagers.

'The same Ram who carried me to the hospital and who is now standing before me.'

The sadhu's consciousness was imbued in bhakti. He was seeing his Lord Ram in all things and relating all events to Him. This is an example of divine thinking.

When our thinking is permeated with God consciousness, we add God to every activity we undertake. For example, while interacting with people, we think:

–   *'God is sitting inside this person. I must not harm him.'*

–   *'God loves her, just as He loves me. So, I should deal with her respectfully.'*

–   *'Like me, this person is also a fraction of God. His soul is also on a journey to the Supreme since endless lifetimes.'*

In our works too, we must keep divine consciousness. A few examples of such thoughts are:

–   *'My profession is not a drudgery but a service to the Divine.'*

–   *'My work is a duty bestowed upon me by God. Let me do it sincerely, for His pleasure.'*

— 'The fruits of my works are not for me but for the Lord. So, I will do my best and leave the rest to God.'

The way we look at the world also changes:

— 'The whole world has emanated from God. There is nothing to abhor in it.'

— 'All I possess belongs to Him. I should give up the pride of ownership.'

— 'The world is made from maya, which is an energy of God. I will keep divine sentiments towards all things.'

Our sense of self-identity and self-purpose also get clarification in following ways:

— 'My self-worth does not come from what others think of me. I am a divine soul and a tiny part of God.'

— 'All I do is by the grace of God. So, I must not be proud of my achievements.'

— 'Life is a gift to me by the Supreme. I must use it well to fulfil the purpose for which I have come to this world.'

These are just a few examples. As we can see, sadhana bhakti does a complete bypass surgery of our thought processes.

And it does not stop there. When purification of the mind is complete, then by the grace of God and Guru, one gets *Prem Shakti, the* divine *Yogmaya* power. At that point, complete union with God takes place.

bhidyate hṛidayagranthiśh
  chhidyante sarva sanśhayāḥ
kṣhīyante chāsya karmāṇi
  tasmindṛiṣhṭe parāvare (*Muṇḍakopaniṣhad* 2.2.8)

This verse states that at the moment of God-realization, one has darshan of the Lord, the bonds of maya are untied, all doubts are dispelled, and the karmas of endless lifetimes are destroyed.

Every thought of such a God-realized soul unites with Him in love. This is the perfectional stage of divine thinking. The *Narad Bhakti Darshan* states: 'On being situated in bhakti, one sees only God; one hears and talks only about God; and one thinks only of God.' (sutra 35).

At that stage, the Supreme Divine Personality becomes a servant of the soul. **Such is the power of thoughts that when correctly used, they can captivate God.** There is so much more to be said about bhakti, but it is beyond the scope of this book.

In this way, our journey through the book that began with the removal of negative thinking has culminated with divine thinking. We have traversed the journey of thoughts from the negative to the positive, from the material to the spiritual, and finally to the divine. The final chapter of this book presents some meditations for your practise.

14

Meditations for Practice

Meditation is not alien to us. We all know how to meditate. A composer meditates day and night on the notes in his music. A writer meditates on the plot unfolding in his mind. A drunkard meditates on the relief the next bottle of whisky will provide to his troubled mind. And a lover meditates on his beloved. These are all examples of the mind naturally focusing on the subject of its attachment.

How is meditation—as a part of yogic practice—distinct from these? It is the subject we meditate upon that makes all the difference. Focusing the mind on a mundane subject makes our consciousness material. In contrast, contemplating a divine subject makes the mind divine.

Shree Krishna states in the Bhagavad Gita:

māṁ cha yo 'vyabhichāreṇa bhakti-yogena sevate
sa guṇān samatītyaitān brahma-bhūyāya kalpate
(verse 14.26)

'Those who absorb their mind in Me with unalloyed devotion rise above the three modes of material nature. Their mind becomes pure, like God Himself.'

Hence, dhyan (meditation) does not mean concentration alone. It is a powerful technique for elevating our consciousness to the Divine.

Benefits of Meditation

Innumerable experiences are stored in our subconscious mind. Dhyan provides us the tools to go deep within and cleanse the mind.

Meditation can help us accomplish the following goals:

- To rein the unbridled mind.

- To use the controlled thought energy to attain our desired goal.

- To develop a strong resolve to attain even difficult goals.

- To cut bad *sanskārs* and habits.

- To develop good personality traits.

- To maintain balance in the midst of adverse circumstances.

- To remain happy in all situations.

- To influence the environment with our positive thoughts.

The ultimate goal of dhyan is God-realization. When the personality of the meditator begins to be illuminated by the divine consciousness of God, then dhyan can be considered to be successful. Meditation, hence, is not a mere state of thoughtlessness; it is the bathing of our personality in elevating thoughts. Here are a few meditations for your practise.

1. Meditation on Noble Thoughts

The goal of this meditation is to develop divine virtues, such as tolerance, compassion, reverence, integrity and so on.

Meditation Steps:

i. Sit cross-legged or in any comfortable posture. If sitting on the floor is uncomfortable for you, seat yourself on a chair.

ii. Keep your back and neck straight.

iii. Close your eyes for the period of the meditation.

iv. Relax your body and calm your mind.

v. Begin breathing deeply. Observe the breath as it flows in from the nostrils into the lungs, and from the lungs out through the nostrils.

vi. After a few breaths, shift your awareness to your chest and stomach. Observe them expanding with the incoming breath and contracting with the outgoing breath.

vii. Visualize the image of Radha Krishna, or any other form of God you worship, in front of you. Now your mind is focused on the Divine.

viii. Think that the Lord is an ocean of infinite tranquillity. Feel peace and tranquillity radiating from Him. Feel tranquillity slowly overtaking your senses and filling your inner self. *Om śhāntiḥ śhāntiḥ śhāntiḥ*

Now meditate on how tolerant God is. He is the Protector of countless souls and knows each soul's every thought. Yet, He does not get angry or tense. His whole presence radiates harmony, serenity and peace. Perceive infinite tolerance in the Lord and then perceive yourself receiving it from Him and absorbing it within you. You are becoming tolerant. No matter how irritating anyone may be, it will have no effect on you, because you have become even more tolerant than a tree.

One of the finest virtues to possess is humility. You are now learning to be humble and gentle with everyone. You take great pleasure in honouring others but do not seek fame yourself. You feel humbler in the presence of the Almighty God, Who is the humblest of all.

The Lord is the Repository of all divine qualities. Meditate that He is before you, and His divine virtues are flooding your mind and body. Meditate that as the good qualities grow within you, negative thoughts and feelings are leaving your personality. Hatred, resentment, etc., are leaving your body. Your mind is becoming endowed with virtues. Clean and pure.

Your mind is becoming as clear as a mountain stream and perfectly balanced. It has lost all the bad thoughts and is now thinking only of the Lord. Slowly, you begin feeling the Lord's grace, and a sense of gratefulness starts to flow through your body. It is due to the Lord's grace that all your negative feelings have gone away, and you feel so good and positive. You have never felt this good before. Feel humble before God and see Him smile back at you.

Consider the people around you, many of them leading a sad and dejected life. Just like you, they are children of God, but they do not realize it.

Pray to the Lord that He brings them on the right path and graces them so that they can follow Him truthfully and sincerely.

These good feelings in you give immense pleasure to the Lord as He now sees you as a changed person with all the divine qualities taking seed in your thoughts. Continue to feel positive and pray to the Lord for the well-being of this whole world.

sarve bhavantu sukhinaḥ
sarve santu nirāmayāḥ
sarve bhadrāṇi paśhyantu
mā kaśhchid duḥkhabhāg bhavet
om śhāntiḥ śhāntiḥ śhāntiḥ

ix. We will now bring the meditation to a close. Gently rub your palms together and place your palms on your eyes. Gently rubbing your eyes with your fingers, open them.

2. Meditation to Develop Gratitude

The most powerful way of countering negative thinking is to develop a deep sense of gratefulness. The sentiment of gratitude shifts our focus away from the dearth in our life to the many blessings we have received. The aim of this meditation is to help us contemplate those graces and enhance the feeling of deep thankfulness in our heart.

Meditation Steps:

i.   Sit cross-legged or in any comfortable posture. If sitting on the floor is uncomfortable for you, seat yourself on a chair.

ii. Keep your back and neck straight.

iii. Close your eyes for the period of the meditation.

iv. Relax your body and calm your mind.

v.   Begin breathing deeply. Observe the breath as it flows in from the nostrils into the lungs, and from the lungs out through the nostrils.

vi. Now let us focus on deepening the virtue of gratitude within ourselves.

Become aware of the air you breathe. It is a gift of God. Create the sentiment that as you breathe in, you are ingesting the grace of the Lord. Thank Him for it with all your heart.

Take your mind to the mother earth that you sit upon. The fertile land, mountains and valleys were all made by the Lord. The soil produces a variety of fruits, grains and vegetables that keep us healthy and nourished. What we eat transforms into blood, flesh, muscle, bone and marrow within our body. Hence, through the earth, the Lord has bestowed many blessings upon us. Feel gratitude towards Him for it.

Imagine that it is morning, and you are watching the sun rising in the east. Its rays are dispelling the darkness of the night. Birds have begun their chirping at the very first sight of light. Contemplate upon the effulgence of the sun that spreads throughout the solar system. See the light that emanates from the sun as a form of God's grace. Visualize yourself standing in the sun and imagine yourself being anointed with grace.

Now look upon your own body. This has also been created by divine grace. When you were an embryo in your mother's womb for nine months, He protected you there. Today you are a grown person, and your body is working because of His grace as well. Observe your tireless heart. It beats 1,00,000 times a day. The blood it pumps reaches every cell of your body through arteries and capillaries. Is it not astonishing?

Your digestive system includes a liver, kidneys, pancreas, etc. All these work in harmony to ensure you continue to receive the gift of life. Visualize them all radiating in good health. They are all engaged in your service. This amazing body you have received is a gift from God. Feel gratitude in your heart for it.

You have received eyes with the power to see. You have been given ears with the power to hear.

Your tongue possesses the power of taste, the skin the power to feel. All these abilities have been bestowed by your Creator, Who is the Source of these powers. Give thanks to Him for these benedictions.

Become aware of the presence of the Lord within your heart. He has been accompanying you since endless lifetimes and is your closest Relative. He notes your karmas and bestows the fruits. He is your eternal Well-Wisher and can do you no harm.

Give thanks to Him. 'O Shree Krishna! I am grateful for all Your graces. You are all-auspicious, and whatever happens by Your grace is also auspicious, though I do not always understand it. I convey my gratitude to You. I am grateful for Your infinite mercies. I will remain ever indebted for them. Thank You, Thank You, Thank You.'

vii. We will now bring the meditation to a close. Gently rub your palms together and place your palms on your eyes. Gently rubbing your eyes with your fingers, open them.

3. Meditation on the Greatness of God

We are endowed with five senses, through which we grasp taste, touch, smell, sight and sound. Interestingly, these five senses reside in the subtle form in our mind. That is how we can see dreams when we sleep. With which eyes do we see dreams? Our eyes are closed and under the bed sheet.

Interestingly, the eyes also reside in the subtle form in the mind. So do all the other senses. Hence, even in the dream state, we can taste, touch, feel, hear and see. In this meditation, we shall be using these five subtle senses. The dream is seen without conscious effort. But in this meditation, we will consciously create the dream state.

Meditation Steps:

i.   Sit cross-legged or in any comfortable posture. If sitting on the floor is uncomfortable for you, seat yourself on a chair.

ii. Keep your back and neck straight.

iii. Close your eyes for the period of the meditation.

iv. Relax your body and calm your mind.

v.   Begin breathing deeply. Observe the breath as it flows in from the nostrils into the lungs, and from the lungs out through the nostrils.

vi. After a few breaths, shift your awareness to your chest and stomach. Observe them expanding with the incoming breath and contracting with the outgoing breath.

vii. The world is full of God's magical creation and every atom of it manifests glimpses of His innumerable glories. Visualize yourself in a beautiful garden with lush green grass and flower beds. It is surrounded by rows of majestic trees.

It is dawn, and the sun is rising. See how soft and beautiful the morning sun is as it rises from the horizon and slowly turns into a fireball. Observe the beautiful birds whose noisy but cheerful calls wake up all. There are some birds that make melodic sounds and attract the attention of their mates. Listen to their sounds and how perfect their calls are. See how many colourful birds God has created. Each bird has a unique body, colour and features. You can see green parrots, black crows and grey pigeons. Now you spy a couple of milk-white swans flying past. Look at how gracefully and swiftly the swans move across the sky. These birds are so elegant. How do they manage it? God has bestowed on them such beauty, grace and poise. What a sight!

A peacock and peahen have appeared in the garden. Look at the peacock. It has such a long and exquisitely feathered tail, unmatched anywhere in the living world. See how it dances in front of its mate. Look at its open feathered tail in iridescent green, indigo, violet, purple and gold. How did the peacock learn to dance so gracefully? Why did God give such a beautiful tail to a peacock and not any other bird? God has inconceivable ways of expressing beauty.

We have all seen butterflies fluttering around in the garden. What a riot of colours in them! From flower to flower, they jump in search of the intoxicating nectar they love dearly. Watch them fold their wings and open them as they devour the nectar from the flowers. It seems like butterflies have been artistically painted from a palette of a million colours. Their carefree flight appears to represent and celebrate God's unbounded joy and happiness.

Now, look at the green trees around the garden; how huge and protective they are. They are souls who are standing upside down with their heads down and legs up in the air! They stand there for years together, providing shelter for those who seek protection under their mighty branches. These life-giving trees consume unclean air and produce fresh oxygen for us to breathe. What a selfless service they perform, though we do not even realize it. We use and abuse them, yet they stand there, silently tolerating us. We sure have something to learn from the selfless benevolence of these trees.

How refreshed we feel looking at the natural wonders around us. The beautiful sunrise, the birds soaring across the horizon. Beyond the garden are beautiful meadows with rich grass for the cattle to feed on. On the horizon are mountains covered with forests as far as the eye can see, snow-laden peaks piercing the clouds to kiss the sky and gentle streams merging to create mighty rivers that unite with the ocean. What natural wonders God has created!

Look at the vast oceans of the world. Endless waves are born that lash the shores, day and night. So mighty and strong, yet they are so contained within their boundaries. Under the turbulent waters thrives a deafening and vibrant world, full of creatures big and small. How astonishing the underwater world is! We hardly know anything about it. Imagine, how big and immeasurable the Creator of this whole universe could be! The Creator of innumerable earths, suns and moons is within us that we still cannot know Him. Astonishing! How could we even think of understanding God, Who created this universe by just wishing it? Our limited intellect is inadequate even to comprehend aspects of this material world, then how can we attempt to comprehend matters beyond its reach. To know God, we will need His grace and mercy. Only then can we begin to understand everything related with creation and beyond.

God has given each living creature a special gift and a unique quality. A dog is so faithful, and it can even sacrifice its life for his master. The honeybees work tirelessly day and night to fill jars of honey for us humans to consume. Cows are known for their soft and calm nature. Horses have tremendous power and can run for miles with a heavy weight behind them. God has created each animal with a lot of thought so that they can be of some use to us. We, humans, are forever indebted to God for the countless graces He has showered on us, yet we remain unfaithful and forgetful of His greatness.

Human life is an opportunity and a priceless gift, not a burden to carry. We must not squander it by thinking negatively, feeling depressed and discouraged or harbouring detrimental emotions within ourselves. This human life has been given to us with a special purpose. We must utilize every moment of our lives for the fulfilment of that purpose and nothing else. The Vedas say, 'O! Humans, arise and awake, do not fall down and squander this chance but move ahead and accomplish your goal. Seek the mercy and grace of a God-realized Saint and learn about the Absolute Truth from Him.'

viii. We will now bring the meditation to a close. Gently rub your palms together and place your palms on your eyes. Gently rubbing your eyes with your fingers, open them.

4. Meditation to Increase Longing for God

In search of happiness, we create countless desires that we think will satisfy our senses and mind. Yet, we do not seem to have attained the ever-elusive happiness that eternally overcomes all the sadness and suffering in our lives. The state of our inner and private world has remained the same, for we constantly harbour desires, anger, disappointment, greed, jealousy, anxiety, lust and other mental ailments. Yet, we remain optimistic that one day, peace and happiness will arrive on a magic carpet, ready to sweep us away to a world of fulfilled desires and never-ending material comforts. Astonishing!

The Vedas inform us that the ocean of happiness is God. To develop an appreciation for the true meaning of happiness and the way to attain it, let us start by diverting our material desires towards the Names, Forms, Virtues, Associates and Pastimes of God. Practising this regularly will help us fix our mind on Him firmly. The more we attach our mind on God, the more we get detached from mundane things, and our hearts will be cleansed to the same proportion.

Meditation Steps:

i. Sit cross-legged or in any comfortable posture. If sitting on the floor is uncomfortable for you, seat yourself on a chair.

ii. Keep your back and neck straight.

iii. Close your eyes for the period of the meditation.

iv. Relax your body and calm your mind.

v. Begin breathing deeply. Observe the breath as it flows in from the nostrils into the lungs, and from the lungs out through the nostrils.

vi. After a few breaths, shift your awareness to your chest and stomach. Observe them expanding with the incoming breath and contracting with the outgoing breath.

vii. Imagine that you have just arrived in *Golok*, the divine Abode of Lord Krishna. Picture the beautiful things that you see in *Golok*. The lush greenery, the cows grazing in the meadows far and wide, birds chirping, the peacocks calling and a stream flowing lethargically like a well-fed snake. As this is the divine Abode, everything here has a special significance. The warm fragrance of the divine trees brushes your nostrils and elevates your senses to a new level.

As you take a stroll, your ears are instantly captivated by a hypnotic melody being played over the hills and far away. Deeply attracted and mesmerized by the divine tunes, imagine yourself being magically transported in the direction of the tantalizing notes. You wonder who could be playing such a wonderful instrument and realize that this divine music is being played by none other than your Soul Beloved, Shree Krishna. You are now running in the direction of the music, stumbling over mounds, wading through ankle-deep water and across the green meadows.

The music gets closer and sweeter, your heart beats faster, but you still can't see Him. You plead with Him to reveal a glimpse of His true self. His divine melody has all but captured your breath.

At that very instant, you think of your beloved Spiritual Master and beg Him to show you a glimpse of Shree Krishna. You pray at His lotus feet to shower His grace upon you so that you can meet your Soul Beloved.

Your Guru agrees to your prayers and offers His reassuring hands, which you gladly hold on to as if your life depends on it. Slowly you gather yourself and follow your Guru in the direction of the soothing notes. Accompanying the melodic flute is the graceful tune emanating from the anklets of Shree Krishna. Unable to comprehend or digest the sweetness of this divine music, you resist the urge to ask your Guru to go faster.

As you scan the horizon, your eyes fall upon the divine river, Yamuna, flowing silently across grassy meadows. The crystal-clear water attracts your attention, but you remain unmoved. Your revered Guru gestures at you as your gaze reaches the divine *kadamb* tree on the banks of the river. Nearby, standing on the tender grass, wearing a silken, yellow cloth, *pītāmbar*, and holding the flute in both His hands, is your Soul Beloved Shree Krishna.

Your eyes cannot believe that Shree Krishna is indeed in front of you, playing the most attractive melodies. Shree Krishna gestures at your Guru to bring you closer to Him. As your Guru steps towards you with His arms wide open, look at yourself fall at His feet and then embrace Him. Tears roll down your cheeks in humble submission to your revered Guru with whose grace this auspicious moment has arrived. He then hands you over to your Beloved Lord, Shree Krishna, Who waits patiently for you to step forward.

Taking permission from your Guru, you are drawn closer to Shree Krishna like a moth is to light. Behold the Lord with all your eyes, for this is the ultimate moment of your life. You have been blessed and graced with the greatest of all boons and the most priceless of all treasures there is or will ever be. The most awaited day of your entire existence has now arrived, for you have a private audience with the Lord Himself!

You now witness Shree Krishna's *roop mādhurī*, or the nectar flowing from His divine form, due to which the Lord of lords appears the most beautiful and handsome. As you lift your head and look into His eyes pouring with love, and a gaze that pierces your heart with a thousand arrows, tears of joy cascade down your cheeks. Your voice is choked, throat dry, and you are unable to utter much. Your eyes now fall upon His admirable crown made of peacock feathers, perched perfectly on His tender head. The feathers fluttering in the gentle breeze appear to fan His soft and curly hair. Your eyes are drawn lovingly to His perfectly formed eyes that resemble that of a peacock feather eye. You are now looking at the prominent tilak on His forehead anointed so expertly.

Shree Krishna is wearing the divine *vaijayantī mala*, a garland made of the choicest of divine flowers, whose fragrance fills the air. Every flower in the garland seems to reach out towards Shree Krishna's nostrils, trying to impress Him with their exotic effervescence. Decked in the choicest of jewellery and the exquisite *Kaustubh Maṇi*, Shree Krishna looks extremely attractive. His trunk is partially covered in the softest of silk dupattas that seem to gently kiss His skin so as to not pain His soft and delicate body. He is draped in yellow cloth, held around His slender waist by a gold band. Your Beloved wears silver anklets that sing as He steps towards you. The sound of the anklets rings in your ears like a symphony of a hundred musicians, elevating your joy to unknown heights.

Shree Krishna now plays the flute, drowning you deeper in the bliss of divine love for your Beloved. Slowly and steadily, you and your Guru move towards Shree Krishna's feet, where you take your rightful place.

As He stands tall, you watch the grass gently support His tender feet and go head over heels to massage them. Every object and living being that you see is doing its best to be of service to Shree Krishna. Your concentration is now on His feet as you thank Him and your Guru profusely for this most fortunate event of your life. Pray to Shree Krishna to grace you in such a way that your permanent place will remain at His lotus feet in eternal service for His happiness alone. Realize yourself to be the humblest of all souls. Shed tears of repentance for His happiness and wash His feet lovingly for His comfort.

Think of yourself to be the most fallen soul and beg for His forgiveness. Fill your heart with love for Shree Krishna. Seeing that His devotee has truly surrendered himself, Shree Krishna now lifts you with His arms and embraces you with all His heart. When you thought that the ultimate joy had been attained, your beloved now fills your heart with more divine love and bliss that is countless times higher than what you received earlier. Shree Krishna Himself is pleased with your selfless love and showers more of His divine love upon you. The tears in your eyes have now formed a constant stream and cleansed your heart forever.

Shree Krishna now instructs your Guru to take you back to earth and asks you if you will continue to love Him more than ever. Reluctantly, you leave His arms and again prostrate at His feet. Shree Krishna again flashes His bewitching smile and says, 'I shall never leave you even for a moment. I am always with you and in you. Think of Me at all times, and you shall be eternally blissful.'

With these words, Shree Krishna bids adieu. Your lovelorn eyes are still filled with tears as you request the Lord for His permission to leave. Shree Krishna sends you off with His blessings as you and your Guru slowly make your way out of Vrindavan. Everything looks pale and lifeless without your Soul-Beloved, but His reassuring words light up your spirits.

Bring yourself back home. Become aware of your body.

viii. We will now bring the meditation to a close. Gently rub your palms together and place your palms on your eyes. Gently rubbing your eyes with your fingers, open them.

5. Meditation to Increase Humility

A humble nature is the hallmark of a mature and noble soul. Humility gives rise to tolerance, happiness, gentleness, lovable behaviour and the feeling of bhakti. The presence of all these qualities in a person makes him or her a balanced, happy and peaceful person. Humility is such a special and unique characteristic that it endears one even to God.

īshvarasyāpyabhimānadveṣhitvād dainyapriyatvāch

(sutra 27)

This verse from the *Narad Bhakti Darshan* says that there is one thing that is dear to God, and that is humility; and there is one thing that He dislikes, and that is pride.

Hence, for our own benefit, we must try to be humble in all our dealings. Let us consciously meditate to increase the feeling of humility within us.

Meditation Steps:

i. Sit cross-legged or in any comfortable posture. If sitting on the floor is uncomfortable for you, seat yourself on a chair.

ii.   Keep your back and neck straight.

iii. Close your eyes for the period of the meditation.

iv.   Relax your body and calm your mind.

v.   Begin breathing deeply. Observe the breath as it flows in from the nostrils into the lungs, and from the lungs out through the nostrils.

vi.   After a few breaths, shift your awareness to your chest and stomach. Observe them expanding with the incoming breath and contracting with the outgoing breath.

vii. Imagine how huge this world is, visualize the grandeur of the great Himalayas. The never-ending snow-capped mountains draped in white and the blue skies providing the perfect background. Pine and deodar forests fill the landscape, and the mighty rivers flow down, creating picture-perfect valleys as they cut through the mountains and meadows. Look at the awe-inspiring mountains in front of you as they reach for the sky. How huge and dominating they are. Compare yourself to these mountains and feel the difference. You are so small and insignificant, but the mountains are so huge and massive.

Bigger and mightier than these mountains are the oceans of the world. Think of the expanse of these oceans and water as far as your eye can see. Oceans span thousands of kilometres, and all you can see around you is water. The loneliness and deafening silence when you are lost at sea is a unique but frightening thought! Smell the moist air blowing as it caresses your face. Look at the waves crash on the shores. Countless drops of rainwater created these oceans, and it seems like we are smaller than that drop of water!

Larger than the oceans is the earth itself, which holds them together like a huge earthen pot. The turbulent seas seem so uncontrollable and strike fear in the hearts of even the bravest of sailors. But they seem like a child in a mother's lap when they are contained within the earth's protective grasp. How is it possible? How large and mighty could the earth be? Look at the planets, so many times bigger than the earth. They all revolve around the sun in a fixed pattern, as if obeying the sun's orders. How powerful and invincible the sun appears!

The sun is just a tiny dot in the Milky Way galaxy that contains billions of other stars. There are millions of such galaxies in this universe, each with its own sun and a planetary system. Try and imagine the enormity of this creation and realize how insignificant a soul is amidst all this.

Now think that Shree Krishna is in front of you. The Lord, Who revealed the Bhagavad Gita and the

Vedas, the Repository of infinite knowledge, the Ocean of eternal happiness and joy, stands in front of your eyes! Every cell in His body overflows with divine love. Pray to Him with all your heart and soul. 'Oh Lord, please grace me such that I can behold You all the time, please bestow upon me Your divine love.' Shree Krishna says, 'My son, I have been waiting for you since eternity with open arms, but your ego is stopping you from attaining Me. Ego is like a cloud that is hiding you away from Me. I grace such a soul who considers himself the most humble and insignificant. If you want to attain Me and My divine love, see to it that your ego is destroyed.'

Now, pray to God to help you get rid of your own ego and increase the feeling of humility and tolerance within you. 'O Lord! My body, mind and intellect are made of maya and full of faults. This body is a storehouse of decomposed material that needs to be removed frequently. My mind is full of imperfect thoughts and suffers from greed, anger, lust, desire, ego, jealousy and countless other mental problems. My intellect is flawed and covered in a veil of impure and incomplete knowledge.

'Since eternity, my intellect has thought of the material world as its own and tried to seek happiness there. Even after the endless disappointments and unhappiness, my mind and intellect draw me towards the material world. I have still not realized that you are my only Beloved. What makes me so egoistic? Please help me overcome this problem and remove this veil so that I can reach You.

'If there is any trace of goodness in me, it is only due to Your grace and mercy. Not a leaf moves without Your grace. Then how is it possible for me to have any good characteristic without Your grace? In fact, I cannot do anything without Your causeless grace, and even the impossible can be made possible with Your grace. O Giver of life, please have mercy on this insignificant fallen soul and grace me with Your divine love and divine vision! I beg you for a drop of the nectar of divine love that You hold so dearly.'

viii. We will now bring the meditation to a close. Gently rub your palms together and place your palms on your eyes. Gently rubbing your eyes with your fingers, open them.

6. Meditation to Practise the Presence of God

Jagadguru Shree Kripaluji Maharaj has revealed this special form of dhyan or meditation to hasten the process of God-realization for every soul. It is a very flexible form of meditation that can be practised in almost any situation. Normally, we associate God with a temple or a place of worship. But the Vedas declare that God resides in every atom of this universe. Hence, it is not necessary that God must live only in a temple, a church or a mosque. He is everywhere and in every being—living or dead. We will now practise meditating on the fact that God and your Guru are always with you, everywhere.

There are many benefits to this type of meditation, and one can progress very fast towards God by practising it. Our aspirations, attachments and desires bind us to this material world. Our mind continuously thinks of something that is dear or close to our hearts. For example, one person may like money, another likes their wife or husband, whereas another person wants fame and so on. The minds of these people are constantly engaged in thinking about their subject of interest and attachment. With some sincere effort, a person can concentrate the mind on another subject, thereby withdrawing it from the things one is so dearly attached to.

Karm yog meditation helps you fix your mind on God. With this type of meditation, God's power and grace will always be with you. When you feel the presence of God all the time, your conscience will remain alert, and you will stop yourself from performing sinful or harmful actions. If you begin to realize that God is protecting you, then all the fears and inhibitions in your mind will slowly vanish.

Performing karm yog meditation will require patience and persistence. We have to reach a stage where the remembrance of God in all aspects of our daily life becomes easy and a natural part of ourselves. In the beginning, we have to put in a lot of effort to concentrate and fix our mind on God and things related to Him. Slowly but steadily, we will make progress. With continuous practise, meditation will become easier and more enjoyable. Sincere practise is the key. Just as when we learn to ride a bicycle or swim, we have to put in our best effort and leave the rest to God. He will help us come closer to Him if we sincerely follow His path.

Meditation Steps:

i.   Sit cross-legged or in any comfortable posture. If sitting on the floor is uncomfortable for you, seat yourself on a chair.

ii. Keep your back and neck straight.

iii. Close your eyes for the period of the meditation.

iv. Relax your body and calm your mind.

v.   Begin breathing deeply. Observe the breath as it flows in from the nostrils into the lungs, and from the lungs out through the nostrils.

vi. After a few breaths, shift your awareness to your chest and stomach. Observe them expanding with the incoming breath and contracting with the outgoing breath.

vii. You are now seated comfortably in your living room at home. Feel the presence of God next to you. There is no need to visualize His form, but feel in your heart that He is next to you and watching you. Touch His feet and seek His grace such that you will always remember Him and that you shall live your life in His presence at all times. In your mind, perform the *Āratī* of God.

Now think that God is standing behind you and watching your every move. He is in fact your Protector. Imagine, the Creator and Protector of unlimited galaxies and this universe is actually your Protector too! So, what are you worried about? Leave all your negative thoughts and worries with Him and revel in the fact that you are protected by none other than God Himself.

God is now standing next to you and smiling at you. He holds your hand as a symbol of His friendship. Imagine in your mind that you too are holding His hand and consider Him as your Best Friend. As your Closest Associate, you will now share every moment with Him and perform every task in His presence and dedicate it to Him. You shall only perform the task, and the Lord shall have the fruit of each action.

Feel that God is now to your left and watching your actions. Feel His grace and presence. He has now placed His divine hands on your head as if blessing you. Your heart leaps with joy, and at the same time, you feel very grateful to the Lord for His benevolence and grace.

You are now inviting God to grace your house and spend some time with you in leisure. Your Lord readily agrees to your request, and you lead Him to your house. You have Him seated on your sofa and you are sitting on the ground, close to His feet. Soon, you begin to take His advice on matters related to your worldly life and dealings. The Lord replies, 'I will not yet answer questions in person. When you call upon Me with a sincere heart and in isolation, I shall lead you in the right way, and I shall illuminate your intellect, which will guide you on the right path'.

It is a very hot day, and you proceed to take a shower. You also ask God if He would like to take a shower and freshen Himself. God readily agrees to your request like a child wanting to play in a pond. In the shower, you are hesitant with your clothes and uncertain of what to do next. The Lord smiles and says, 'My dear friend, I live in every atom of your body, and I live in your heart. I am everywhere. Why this hesitation? There is nothing

I do not know or cannot see. I have declared in the Bhagavad Gita to remember Me and see Me everywhere. In the temple, at work, while cooking, resting and even in your shower!' Hearing these words, your mind and intellect are cleared of a great flaw and redeemed of a silly inhibition. You feel humbled by His words.

Finishing your shower, you slowly walk towards your living room again accompanied by your Beloved Friend and Lord. Every step you take, He watches you. He knows every breath you take and every move of yours. He is watching you closely and endlessly. You realize this fact and your feeling of loneliness is gone! You now begin to believe what He had said earlier. 'I am always with you. You belong to Me. I am your Father, and you are My child.'

With these words, your spirit feels free as a bird. You fall at His lotus feet and begin to pray. 'Dear Lord, the reason for all problems in my life is that I had forgotten You and was thinking only of matters in the material world. I had turned my back towards You. Now, due to Your grace, I have learnt that only You are mine. I want to make this life successful by surrendering myself completely to You. I shall now attempt to perform every task by remembering You all the time. I shall aim to consider every task as service to You (seva) and to dedicate every action for Your benefit and comfort only. Dear Lord, I beg You to grace me and have mercy on me. Please grace me with Your divine love and service.'

viii. We will now bring the meditation to a close. Gently rub your palms together and place your palms on your eyes. Gently rubbing your eyes with your fingers, open them.

Guide to Hindi Pronunciation

Vowels

अ	*a*	as *u* in 'but'
आ	*ā*	as *a* in 'far'
इ	*i*	as *i* in 'pin'
ई	*ī*	as *i* in 'machine'
उ	*u*	as *u* in 'push'
ऊ	*ū*	as *o* in 'move'
ए	*e*	as *a* in 'evade'
ऐ	*ai*	as *a* in 'mat'; sometimes as *ai* in 'aisle' with the only difference that *a* should be pronounced as *u* in 'but', not as *a* in 'far'
ओ	*o*	as *o* in 'go'
औ	*au*	as *o* in 'pot' or as *aw* in 'saw'
ऋ	*ṛi*	as *ri* in 'Krishna'[1]
ॠ	*ṝī*	as *ree* in 'spree'

Consonants

Gutturals: Pronounced from the throat

क	*ka*	as *k* in 'kite'

---

[1] Across the many states of India, *ṛi* is pronounced as '*ru*' as *u* in push. In most parts of North India, *ṛi* is pronounced as *ri* in Krishna. We have used the North Indian style here.

ख	*kha*	as *kh* in 'Eckhart'
ग	*ga*	as *g* in 'goat'
घ	*gha*	as *gh* in 'dighard'
ङ	*ṅa*	as *n* in 'finger'

Palatals: Pronounced with the middle of the tongue against the palate

च	*cha*	as *ch* in 'channel'
छ	*chha*	as *chh* in 'staunchheart'
ज	*ja*	as *j* in 'jar'
झ	*jha*	as *dgeh* in 'hedgehog'
ञ	*ña*	as *n* in 'lunch'

Cerebrals: Pronounced with the tip of the tongue against the palate

ट	*ta*	as *t* in 'tub'
ठ	*ṭha*	as *th* in 'hothead'
ड	*ḍa*	as *d* in 'divine'
ढ	*ḍha*	as *dh* in 'redhead'
ण	*ṇa*	as *n* in 'burnt'

Dentals: Pronounced like the cerebrals but with the tongue against the teeth

त	*ta*	as *t* in French word 'matron'
थ	*tha*	as *th* in 'ether'
द	*da*	as *th* in 'either'

| ध | *dha* | as *dh* in 'Buddha' |
| न | *na* | as *n* in 'no' |

Labials: Pronounced with the lips

प	*pa*	as *p* in 'pink'
फ	*pha*	as *ph* in 'uphill'
ब	*ba*	as *b* in 'boy'
भ	*bha*	as *bh* in 'abhor'
म	*ma*	as *m* in 'man'

Semi-vowels

य	*ya*	as *y* in 'yes'
र	*ra*	as *r* in 'remember'
ल	*la*	as *l* in 'light'
व	*va*	as *v* in 'vine', as *w* in 'swan'

Sibilants

श	*śha*	as *sh* in 'shape'
ष	*ṣha*	as *sh* in 'show'
स	*sa*	as *s* in 'sin'

Aspirate

| ह | *ha* | as *h* in 'hut' |

Visarga

| : | *ḥ* | it is a strong aspirate; also lengthens the preceding vowel and occurs only at the end of a word. It is pronounced as a final *h* sound |

Anusvara Nasalized

˙	*ṁ/ṅ*	nasalizes and lengthens the preceding vowel and is pronounced as *n* in the words 'and' or 'anthem'[2]
ꣳ	~	as *n* in 'gung-ho'

Avagraha

ऽ	'	This is a silent character indicating अ. It is written but not pronounced; used in specific combination (sandhi) rules

Others

क्ष	*kṣha*	as *ksh* in 'freak show'
ज्ञ	*jña*	as *gy* in 'bigyoung'
ड़	*ṛa*	There is no sign in English to represent the sound ड़. It has been written as *ṛa* but the tip of the tongue quickly flaps down
ढ़	*ṛha*	There is no sign in English to represent the sound ढ़. It has been written as *ṛha* but the tip of the tongue quickly flaps down

---

2 Sometimes nasalized and sometimes not. Many words such as *Aṁsh, Saṁskar*, etc., are pronounced with a nasal sound as *Aṅsh, Saṅskar*, etc. OR Since it is nasalized, we are using *ṅ*.

Glossary

ananya bhakti	exclusive devotion; devotion where the mind is attached exclusively to God and nowhere else in the world
āsakti	clinging of our mind to an object; attachment
atma nirīkṣhaṅ	self-introspection
bhakti	devotion
dhyan	meditation
dveṣh	attachment with negative sentiments such as hatred
gunas	three modes of nature—goodness, passion and ignorance
Jagadguruttam	supreme Spiritual Master of the world
kapha	From the Ayurveda branch of medicine that describes three basic doshas (elements) of the body as: kapha (earth and water), pitta (fire) and vatta (space or air) that need to be in balance for a healthy body
kusaṅg	negative/bad association
nādis	energy channels within the body

niṣhkām bhakti	selfless devotion; devotion that is free from selfish desires
nitya bhakti	continuous devotion; devotion to practise the presence of God at all times
pāvanaṁ pāvanānām	the source of all purity in the world
pitta	see kapha
pran	subtle life force energy that pervades the breath and varieties of animate and inanimate objects
pranic shakti	vital energy or life-airs
pratipakṣha bhāvanā	practice of focusing on an opposite thought
rāg	attachment with positive sentiments such as love
sādhaks	spiritual aspirants
sadhana bhakti	devotion that must be practised to purify our heart. Also called preparatory devotion.
sākṣhī bhāv	a 'state of being the witness'. It refers to the practice of observing sensations in our mind and body without immediately reacting to them.
saṅkalp	to desire something or someone; to hanker for; to long for

sanskārs	accumulated tendencies from endless previous lifetimes
satsang	association that takes our mind to the Absolute Truth
seva	service
shakti	energy
siddha bhakti	grace bestowed by God. Also called perfect devotion.
siddhis	material, paranormal powers, attained when the mind achieves a high level of concentration through yoga and meditation
tamasic	of the mode of ignorance
vatta	see kapha
vikalp	aversion; opposite of sankalp
viparyaya	reversal of intellect leading to opposite or incorrect knowledge
yogmaya	highest bliss-giving power of God; divine power of God

Other Books by the Author

7 Divine Laws to Awaken Your Best Self
7 Mindsets for Success, Happiness and Fulfilment
(Also available in Hindi & Marathi)
Bhagavad Gita, The Song of God
Essence of Hinduism
Science of Healthy Diet
Spiritual Dialectics
The Science of Mind Management
(Also available in Gujarati & Telugu)
Yoga for Body, Mind & Soul

Books for Children
Festivals of India
Healthy Body, Healthy Mind: Yoga for Children
Inspiring Stories for Children (set of 4 books)
Mahabharat: The Story of Virtue and Dharma
My Best Friend Krishna
My Wisdom Book: Everyday Shlokas, Mantras, Bhajans and More
Ramayan: The Immortal Story of Duty and Devotion
Saints of India

Let's Connect

If you enjoyed reading this book and would like to connect with Swami Mukundananda, you can reach him through any of the following channels:

Websites: *www.jkyog.org, www.jkyog.in, www.swamimukundananda.org*

YouTube channels: 'Swami Mukundananda' and 'Swami Mukundananda Hindi'

Facebook: 'Swami Mukundananda' and 'Swami Mukundananda Hindi'

Instagram: 'Swami Mukundananda' and 'Swami Mukundananda Hindi'

LinkedIn: Swami Mukundananda

Pinterest: Swami Mukundananda - JKYog

Podcasts: Apple, Google, SoundCloud, Spotify, Stitcher

Telegram: Swami Mukundananda

Twitter: Swami Mukundananda (@Sw_Mukundananda)

JKYog Radio: TuneIn app for iOS (Apple App Store) and Android (Google Play Store)

JKYog App: Available for iOS (Apple App Store) and Android (Google Play Store)

WhatsApp Daily Inspirations: We have two broadcast lists. You are welcome to join either or both.

USA: +1 346-239-9675

India: +91 84489 41008

Online Classes:

JKYog India: www.jkyog.in/online-sessions

JKYog USA: www.jkyog.org/online-classes

Email: deskofswamiji@swamimukundananda.org

To bring *The Power of Thoughts* or Swami Mukundananda to your organization—as Google, Intel, Oracle, Verizon, United Nations, Stanford University, Yale University, IITs and IIMs have—please write to deskofswamiji@swamimukundananda.org